Also by Mim Chapman:

Music in Our Society
Music for Today
Recorder Teaching
I Know You Love Challenges…
Open Letter from a Dreamer to an Administrator
The Aleknagik Project, A Success Story of Cooperative School Restructuring
Beyond Gender Stereotypes
A Brief Visual Outline for Successful Lesson Planning
The Future Search Retreat
WHAT IF? Rethinking Education
The VP (vagina-penis) Dialogues, A Sex Education Performance Arts Piece

WHAT DOES POLYAMORY LOOK LIKE?

*Polydiverse Patterns of Loving and Living
in Modern Polyamorous Relationships*

Mim Chapman, PhD

with a forward by Alice Ladas, EdD, co-author of *The G-Spot*

iUniverse, Inc.
New York   Bloomington

What Does Polyamory Look Like?
Polydiverse Patterns of Loving and Living in Modern Polyamorous Relationships

MIMCO
Santa Fe, New Mexico
www.mimco.org

iUniverse books may be ordered through booksellers or by contacting:

iUniverse
1663 Liberty Drive
Bloomington, IN 47403
www.iuniverse.com
1-800-Authors (1-800-288-4677)

ISBN: 978-1-4502-2008-8 (pbk)
ISBN: 978-1-4502-2009-5 (ebk)

Printed in the United States of America

iUniverse rev. date: 7/30/2010

To Navin Sharma,
my brave, creative, loving friend
who has dedicated his life to fighting discrimination,
challenging people in high places to understand and respect diversity,
thus making the world a safer, more accepting place for us all.

Contents

Illustrations

Foreword
by Alice Kahn Ladas, EdD

As a psychologist, with a specialty in Body Psychotherapy, who has been working in the field of sexual education, therapy and research for more than fifty years, I am happy to see more information about polyamory becoming available.

It is not relevant whether one is for or against poly. It exists all around us, whether we like it or not. We pillory our leaders (whether in politics, sports, or entertainment) and our next-door neighbors for not adhering to the cultural icon of life-long monogamy. How much more humane and credible it would be if we acknowledged that monogamy works for some people and not for others. Yet heterosexual monogamy is the only officially sanctioned form of romantic partnership in our Western culture.

Many of us human beings practice serial monogamy. Others "cheat" on their spouses. Today the divorce rate in the United States is around fifty percent, if not higher. Divorce is always disruptive, even when it does not involve acrimony. Often it is traumatizing to the children as well as to the couples involved. Wouldn't it be better if we considered how to achieve what we think we want or believe we need in less hurtful ways? How much more loving it might be to practice inclusion, rather than exclusion. But also, how much more challenging, time consuming, as well as growth promoting inclusion can be. If honesty and communication are keys to successful poly, they are also keys to living a successful, loving life of any style. Might it be wiser to discuss relationship options openly rather than to make commitments we may not want or be able to keep?

Mim's book is delightfully lighthearted, inclusively descriptive, and relevantly self-revealing. You really understand where she is coming from, who and what helped her get there and where she wants us to go in our understanding of this often misunderstood lifestyle. She clarifies the distinction between polyamory and promiscuity, polygamy and swinging. The latter is primarily about sexual connections, whereas poly is about expanding one's circle of intimate, loving, relationships in ways that may or may not include sexuality.

The book is an important resource for people involved or thinking about becoming involved in some form of polyamory. It is also an excellent source of information for professionals of all kinds (e.g. psychologists, ministers, psychiatrists, social workers) who counsel people about relationship issues. It provides useful information about non-traditional options which can help readers to make more informed, intentional choices.

Alice K. Ladas, Ed.D, is co-author of The New York Times bestseller, "The G Spot and Other Discoveries About Human Sexuality." She is a Licensed Psychologist in New Mexico and New York; a Certified Bioenergetic Therapist; a National Health Service Provider in Psychology; a Diplomate in Sexual Therapy and Social Work; a board member of the United States Association for Body Psychotherapy formerly in charge of research; and a Humanist Celebrant.

Introduction

Welcome to this casual discussion of one of my favorite subjects – LOVE, in all its varied forms! You must also be a fan of love, or you wouldn't have joined us by picking up this little book.

Let's start by getting acquainted. I already know a few things about you. You're obviously open-minded, creative, and interested in the subject of love. Maybe you're longing to have more love in your life, or maybe you have so much love in your life that you need help figuring out how to organize your time to fit it all in! You may already identify as polyamorous, and may have been in some type—or several types—of polyamorous relationships even longer than I have. Or you may be new to polyamory, and eager to learn as much as possible about the many options awaiting you within this exciting but sometimes confusing lifestyle.

You may be happily single with no intention of forming a major partnership, but that doesn't necessarily mean that you don't like having love in your life. Or you may be single and dating, contemplating what you really want in a relationship. You may be in a new relationship in which you're fantasizing and pondering about what type of life commitments you want to make. This is a great time to look at various options so you can make conscious, informed choices rather than just signing up for the Sears Roebuck standard model of family because it's there, you're familiar with it, and it's the one your parents had. Some people simply buy the car their dad drove, but most folks spend time looking around the lot to check out what makes and models are available and what features best fit their tastes and needs. Isn't your romantic relationship more important than your car?

Some of you are currently in a monogamous relationship but contemplating opening it up to include other loves, and wondering how that might work for you. Maybe your partner has suggested opening up your currently monogamous relationship, and you're not sure if that's a good idea, or can't quite visualize what life would look like with additional lovers involved with one or both of you. You may be, quite frankly, terrified at the very notion.

Maybe you've tried poly and it didn't work for you, but you like some aspects of the concept and are curious as to whether there are other ways you might have created and organized your relationship, or future relationships, that would work better for you.

Perhaps you've heard the word but can't quite picture what polyamory is, or how it works in real life. Or you might have a friend or family member who is in a relationship with more than one person and you'd like to learn how such a weird arrangement works, but don't want to ask probing questions.

You might be a person who is interested in polyamory professionally rather than personally. You could be a social worker, therapist, counselor, health care provider, or minister who is dedicated to providing all of your clients or congregants with the best possible guidance, advice and service, no matter what type of relationship they have. You may not be sure how you'd react, or how well you'd be able to offer understanding and help, if three or more adults, hand in hand, walked into your office or church introducing themselves as a family and seeking your professional service. Or you might be an educator, youth counselor or director of religious education needing to be comfortable working with children in poly families and wanting to offer today's young people a more complete introduction to the many types of relationship options they have out there in the world, so that they can make intelligent, informed choices about the lives they want for themselves.

Finally, you may be a total cynic and think polyamory couldn't possibly work for anyone, or at least not for you. You may even think any form of non-monogamy is downright disgusting, a wicked, lascivious lifestyle you'd like to learn more about so you can argue against it more knowledgably, and warn your children about its evils. Hey, you're more than welcome to our discussion. We don't think poly is the *best* lifestyle, any better than any other honest, loving way of living. And we certainly don't think it's for everyone! If, when you finish reading, you still think we're wicked, awful folks, we'll still respect your freedom to feel that way, our only hope being that you'll understand us a bit better, whether or not you accept us and our lifestyle.

Then perhaps you've never heard of polyamory, but are just curious and picked up this book because you liked the illustrations on the cover. Whatever your reasons and whatever your goals, we welcome you to the discussion table.

A short preview map may help you find your way to specific topics. Chapters 3 - 7 focus on five different models of polyamory. Each of these chapters contains a description of the relationship type and the following sub-topics: some advantages and challenges of this form of polyamory; issues that need to be agreed upon; poly etiquette, which is often somewhat different from the more familiar behavior patterns seen in the monogamous world, and may vary among the various styles of polyamory; and ways this model of poly may morph to or from other poly relationship patterns.

Your suggestions and feedback are welcomed. The author would love to hear stories of your own poly relationships, which model(s) you resonate with or are living, what challenges you've overcome, and what makes your form of polyamory work for you. You can contact her at mimco8@gmail.com to share questions, suggestions, and your personal "Poly Success Stories," hopefully with your permission to use them (without names, of course) in future poly workshops and presentations. The more we share our stories, the more we realize that although we are pioneers, we are not alone, we do not need to stay in our own little closets, and we can make a difference in the world.

Chapter 1

What is Polyamory?

A Definition and Brief History

What is Polyamory?
A Definition and Brief History

What is Polyamory? Although the lifestyle has existed for thousands of years, the word *polyamory* was created just a few decades ago. It is itself a polylingual word, made up of the Greek word *poly* for many and the Latin word *amor,* love. So polyamory literally means *many loves.* Of course, *many* may be a bit of an overstatement. Most people describe polyamory as a lifestyle based on the belief that one can love more than one person at the same time with honesty, passion, romance, and commitment. You may already know all this, so if you've been practicing a polyamorous lifestyle for years, you may want to skip this chapter, or perhaps just scan it for additional ideas you can use to describe poly the next time *you're* asked to explain it!

The first time I had to formally describe polyamory was in a Sunday morning sermon I was invited to give on the subject at our Unitarian Universalist Fellowship in Anchorage, Alaska. Since this was a Sunday sermon, I decided to start with a Sunday School story. Let's face it, many of our beliefs come from the stories we've been taught from childhood, on Sundays and the rest of the week, so this story makes a good starting point for me when I'm asked to explain polyamory.

So there was Noah, according to the story, building an ark to save life on earth. Who was admitted and sheltered in his ark? Good old Noah and Mrs. Noah, of course, and a pair of each creature: male and female—two by two. Male and female—two by two. Male and female—two by two. And our society, rain or no rain, still maintains those requirements for being accepted into the ark of familial safety, legality, and acceptability: male and female—two by two.

The Gay/Lesbian/Bisexual/Transgender (GLBT) community and their allies are fighting to give male/male and female/female couples the right to enter the ark of social acceptance along with traditional male/female couples. Polyamorists are now taking on the second half of what I call the Noah syndrome, the two by two bit.

Polyamory is a lifestyle based on the belief that it is not only possible but also perfectly normal to love more than one person at the same time. It holds that love is like the light of a candle. If I light your candle, then light a second candle, the second candle does not diminish the light of your candle, nor of mine. In fact, the group of candles can preserve the flame more securely than can any one or two candles alone.

Life, of course, is never as simple as a simile. Polyamorists admit that creating and nurturing multiple relationships is not easy. Polyamory requires massive amounts of communication, trust, honesty, commitment and dedication, as well as a fairly high level of maturity and self-confidence. But who said *any* relationship was easy?

How is polyamory different from swinging? Both value honest nonexclusivity, but that's where the similarity may end. Polyamory is based on freedom to develop *emotional intimacy* with more than one person, sex being a possible outcome but not the primary goal. Swinging, on the other hand, emphasizes sex itself, often having the ground rule that it is okay to have sex with another person so long as you ***don't*** get involved emotionally.

Some people associate *polyamory* with *polygamy*, because both words start with *poly* and refer to non-monogamous relationships. But although the words sound similar, the values and dynamics of polyamory and polygamy are extremely different. In cultures that condone polygamy, one man can own and be married to two or more women. He holds the position of greatest power in his family, and often in his society as a whole. On the other hand, polyamory is not based on ownership. Some people postulate that this is one reason poly is not yet very well accepted in our culture, since ownership is a strong, key value in capitalism. Poly families often contain multiple partners of both genders, and members share power equally, collaborating in making decisions that are mutually beneficial, rather than obeying any one member.

Another popular misconception is that polyamory is just a fancy word for promiscuity. But notice that the word is poly*amory*, not poly*sexuality*. Loving more than one in no way infers loving anyone and everyone, or jumping into bed with as many people as possible. In fact, some people jest that poly folks are so busy communicating and becoming emotionally intimate that there's no time or energy left for mere sex! I can assure you that this is not true. But polyamorists do focus on building a loving community, not just on finding multiple partners to frolic with sexually. We love to frolic, but find that love and honesty make sex way juicier!

I've heard people ask if polyamory provides an escape from intimacy and commitment. Any experienced poly person will attest to the fact that creating poly relationships requires even more intimacy, commitment, courage, negotiation and open communication than many traditional relationships. Poly is based on genuine friendship, mutual respect, and a challenging balance between personal freedom and collaborative responsibility.

What does a poly relationship look like? It has been said that there are as many kinds of polyamorous relationships as there are polyamorists. Some look like the good old-fashioned "open marriage," whether the primary partners are gay or straight. Then there are polyfidelity families – groups of three, four, five or more people who have a long-term commitment to each other and are sexually exclusive within the group. Polyfamilies may include gay, straight, and bi members. Many were formed specifically to provide extended family for their children. Another common relationship form is the intimacy chain sometimes called a Z, N, or W after the shape of the capital letters, i.e., a Z relationship might be made up of Alex+Britt, Britt+Casey, and Casey+Drew with no particular intimacy among the entire group, although they all know the others exist and may all be friends. Sound confusing? Try adding children and jobs and dating schedules! But the benefits of trading *ownership* for *freedom and diversity* in love relationships more than outweigh the challenges, according to many in the poly community. The purpose of this book is to take a closer look at some of the common patterns that are emerging within this polydiversity of poly relationship patterns.

Critics claim that polyamorous relationships won't last. Well, divorce rates certainly don't speak well for the longevity of monogamous relationships! According to Dr. Deborah Anapol, author of *Polyamory: The New Love Without Limits*, polyamory facilitates longevity because a relationship does not need to end just because a partner develops affection for another person.

She says monogamy, though the only officially sanctioned relationship model in our culture, is in actuality seldom practiced. True, there are couples that fall in love and maintain a happy, loving, exciting monogamous relationship for their entire lives. But many others have relationships that are actually polyamorous but which charade as socially acceptable monogamy. The first she calls serial monogamy—loving many people but across time, as in *I love only you; we break up and it's over. Now I love only YOU; then we break up. And now I love only* **YOU***, etc.* Another is monogamy in name only—monogamy with a wee bit of cheating: *I love only YOU, but I sneak around to love him, and if YOU ever find out, there'll be hell to pay!* The former causes the pain of serial break-ups; the latter the pain, guilt, and lack of intimacy that comes from dishonesty, not to mention fear of getting caught. The upfront work involved in creating and maintaining a polyamorous relationship is intense, but it is also positive, honest, and constructive.

Of course, more than two is not new. Polygamy (one man, several women) as practiced in the Old Testament, in Mormonism, and in parts of the Islamic, African and Arab world, is a patriarchal system where a man rules his harem—the extreme ownership situation. In contrast, polyamory focuses on creating egalitarian relationships where all members have equal authority and responsibility. Polyamory is non-hierarchical, and this makes it quite different from more traditional monogamous and non-monogamous relationships.

Although we hear more about polygamy in other parts of the world and other cultures, polyandry (one woman with several husbands) is also part of a number of cultures. I love the story in Hindu scripture about the woman who prayed to Shiva asking for a husband who was handsome, a husband who was kind, one who was intelligent, loving, wealthy. So Shiva answered her prayer and gave her a husband who was handsome, his brother who was kind, their brother who was intelligent, the fourth who was loving, and the wealthy fifth. She lived happily with her five husbands, according to the Sanskrit story. On my recent visit to Tibet, I found that even today it is not unusual for a woman to have more than one husband, and in other families for a man to have more than one wife. So more than one is not new.

For that matter, although I have never heard a sermon preached on the topic, according to the Old Testament, the three major religions of the western world came from a polyamorous Triad—Abraham, Sarah, and Hagar. As we all probably remember, Abraham and Sarah gave birth to Isaac from whom came the Jewish tribes, from whence came Christ and Christianity, while

Abraham and Hagar gave birth to Ishmael from whom came the Arabic nations, Mohammad and Islam. So Christians, Muslims and Jews all owe their heritage to polyamory! That's one you can quote to the next person who tells you how wild, wicked, and against their religion the polyamorous lifestyle is.

The Old Testament is full of stories of non-monogamous families, Abraham and Solomon being among the best known. Both Hinduism and Buddhism, which was an outgrowth of Hinduism, have stories of both polygamy and polyandry. Many Native American stories contain references to non-monogamous relationships. So it is hard to find any basis for the claim that polyamory is against any major religious belief. On the other hand, all major religions hold up honesty as a virtue, so the common societal practice of claiming monogamy while practicing a bit of cheating here and there is not a viable alternative to the honesty that is perhaps the most radical aspect of polyamory.

A number of books focus on the more recent history of polyamory, so this book will do no more than define poly and give a bibliography of books and websites so you may read more on your own. But I've always felt that external history needs to be balanced with personal history. So while defining polyamory, I'll take this time to help you get to know me a bit by describing my own personal history with the topic.

I've always been poly, but I didn't know there was a word to describe my affectional orientation. When I was married, my husband and I decided the nuclear family was a nuclear disaster, or at least we thought it would be for us. "It takes a village to raise a child" is not a new realization, as is evident in the child-rearing practices of a wide variety of cultures throughout history. The idea of two people behind a suburban picket fence trying to raise children all on their own, while both working at demanding professions, is a very modern idea, and one that isn't working very well in many instances. According to Margaret Mead, "Nobody has ever before asked the nuclear family to live all by itself in a box the way we do. With no relatives, no support, we've put it in an impossible situation." She is also reputed to have said that the nuclear family is as deadly as the weapon of the same name!

My husband and I agreed with Margaret Mead. We decided we didn't want to bring children into the world unless we could find or form an extended family to help us raise them, and neither of our blood families were options. We had several intimate relationships with other couples, none of which ended up lasting, and he died at thirty-four, before we found the couple(s) we were seeking, so we had no children.

After his death, I continued my search for an intimate family. Back then, when everyone was reading *The Harrod Experiment* and *Stranger in a Strange Land*, looking for a group to "grok" with was not that unusual. (For you youngsters who missed that era, "grok" meant an erotic, non-possessive heart-connection among a group of like-minded people.) However, as the 70's turned to the 80's and 90's, I began to feel pretty out of place. I had my share of friends and lovers and a handful of viable marriage proposals, each of which I turned down, not because I didn't like the person, but because a traditional marriage just wasn't what I was looking for.

After a while, I started to think that something was wrong with me. Perhaps I needed more therapy, was afraid of commitment, or was fixated on trying to create the family I hadn't had the good fortune to be born into. One by one, my friends marched down the aisle, and I began to believe something about me was really messed up. I felt like the only person in the world who had this weird dream of forming a family of more than two lovers.

Then one fall, I was working on a gay rights campaign in Alaska. One late night, after hours stamping envelopes, we ordered in pizza, put our feet up, and started talking about our personal dreams. I took the risk of sharing mine. I said I could really understand the feelings of some of my older gay friends who'd grown up never even hearing the word "gay," so thought they were the only ones in the world who felt like they did. "There is not even a word for my personal romantic fantasy," I said.

"But there *is* a word for the relationship you dream of—Polyamory!" said the woman from Gay/Lesbian Task Force who was there helping us with the final days of the campaign. "And there are websites, and national gatherings, local discussion groups, and political activists. You're not alone! Just look up www.polyamorysociety.org or www.lovemore.com and you'll find links to lots of groups of people who share your affectional orientation!" Who says there are no personal benefits in working for political causes?

As soon as I got home, I googled *polyamory*, and sure enough, there were gobs of organizations, postings, and meetings all over the world—but none in Alaska! However, at least I knew I was not alone in the world!

I first came out to several of my close gay and lesbian friends as we were on the road to lead a Welcoming Congregation seminar for a rural Unitarian Universalist Fellowship. None of these friends had heard of polyamory, and they had mixed opinions as to whether the GLBT community would be welcoming. One said, "Right now, gays are focusing so hard on winning partnership rights by showing society that we're just like straight couples except for the fact that we're the same gender that it just isn't the right time to mention relationships of more than two people. That's way more scary than gayness!" But another said, "There's never a good time to come out, or a guaranteed safe group to come out to. But if not now, when? And if not us, who?" I will love that woman forever!

I wanted to know more before I said more. That winter I spent several months in New York and went to the meetings of the NY Polyamory Society, held in the big GLBT Center in the Village. I found a wonderful, interesting, welcoming group of people there, people of all sexual orientations, races, and a wide variety of ages. It felt like coming home! I became friends with one of the founders of Unitarian Universalists for Polyamory Awareness. (Leave it to UU's to welcome every stray social radical, right?) Then I went to a Tri-State Poly Munch where I met a couple from the Philly area, and we eventually fell in love. My first poly Triad! What great good fortune! And good fortune it was, because both of them were pros at the art of poly communication and negotiation. Eventually distances and other considerations got in the way of the Triad lasting, although we're still great friends. And I will be forever thankful to them for teaching me so much about the wonderful world of honest communication within non-monogamy.

Several years later, at a west coast polyamory conference, I met a gorgeous young man who was living on his sailboat in Mexico—not a likely match for a woman living in rural Alaska. But magic happens, and the two of us are now living in a beautiful home in Santa Fe, New Mexico where we host the Northern New Mexico Polyamory Network discussion group every month.

So that is a brief tour through a touch of my personal history with poly, and a bit of the world history of the lifestyle. We're not new, we're not rare, and actually, the only thing radical about polyamory is the honesty part. So if you, or friends of yours, are still suffering from the Noah syndrome and thinking, like I did, that you're just weird, sick, or hopelessly out of step with society and will never find what you long for, I hope this chapter provides a bit of encouragement. Hopefully, the rest of the book will help you clarify just what it is that you dream for in a relationship.

Before ending this introductory chapter, there are a few poly concepts that it may be helpful to describe. First, it is important to emphasize that polyamory means *many loves*, not necessarily *many lovers*. I've seen some poly relationship diagrams in which links were drawn only between people who were sexually intimate with each other. Nevertheless, in reality, it is the love between two people who make it a poly relationship, whether or not that love is expressed sexually. For example, there are mixed-gender poly Triads in which the two same-sex members are not bisexual, but an equal love bond exists between each of the three partners of the Triad.

Another core poly concept is that, unlike polygamy or polyandry, polyamory is based on egalitarianism. All members of poly families generally have equal power, responsibility, and input into day-to-day activities as well as larger decisions about the type of relationship they wish to form and the agreements or contracts they negotiate. There may be some modification of this in poly families who also practice some form of BDSM (bondage/discipline, dominance/ submission, sado/masochism). The poly community tends to be quite open and accepting of these and other alternative styles of loving. But equality among all the members of a family tends to be stronger in poly families than in many traditional marriages.

Having said this, it is also important to emphasize that there can be different levels of involvement and commitment between various members of a poly network or family. Some poly folks abhor any type of hierarchy and consider all loves as equal partners. Others use terms like "primary," "secondary," and "tertiary" to describe the difference between major partners and more casual lovers, playmates, friends, or long-distance family members. Primary, secondary, and other partners have equal value, of course, but may not have equal time, commitment or responsibility within a relationship group, and many poly folks like having terms to describe the chosen relationship status of each member in their group.

Compersion is another important poly concept. Some people describe compersion as the opposite of jealousy. Jealousy is based, in part, on a belief in scarcity—I was given only one cup of love, and if I give a spoon of it to him, I have one less spoonful for you! This sense of scarcity breeds envy, fear of loss, and competitiveness. It leads to worrying that if a new love is more attractive, sexier, brighter, or more fun than I am, my primary may leave me for that person, and I'll be all alone once more. Literature and television reinforce this model of scarcity, and sometimes go so far as to see jealousy as an evidence of love! Compersion, on the other hand, is based on a belief in abundance, in which there is no need to compete for the supposedly scarce commodity of love. It holds that love breeds more love, and that when I see someone I love experiencing joy from the love of someone else, this brings me joy as well. It sees jealousy as a sign of insecurity, clinging possessiveness, and greed. When we experience compersion, we celebrate the wealth of love in the world, and find joy in giving and sharing love as a part of a non-competitive, open, non-possessive network.

If, after reading all this, it sounds way too weird for you, and you decide monogamy is what you really want, that's just fine! Remember, polyamory is not just supportive of the concept of having *many loves,* but also supportive of *many ways of loving,* and monogamy is definitely one of those perfectly wonderful ways of loving. Polyamorists envision a world in which people are free to express love in a wide variety of ways, each person finding his or her own most comfortable way of loving others, either within or beyond the existing norms. I hope that reading this book will help us all gain more understanding and respect for each other and the multiple dreams we have, the multiple lives we choose, and the multiple ways we choose to love.

So here's to more loving, and possibly to loving more!

Chapter 2

Polymorphous Diversity

The Array of Designer Relationships in Polyamory

Polymorphous Diversity
The Array of Designer Relationships in Polyamory

Polyamory is sometimes described as many ways of loving, not just many loves. To be totally honest, most of us don't really have all that *many* loves...after all, although love is unlimited, time and emotional energy do have limits! Similarly, there really aren't all that many family formations or ways of loving, but with polyamory comes the freedom, and the challenge, of creating whatever type of relationship works for individual people and their partner(s).

If you're new to poly but have read the first chapter and understand the basic concept, you may now be asking, "But what does polyamory look like?" You've read the definition—a lifestyle based on the belief that one can love more than one person at the same time, honestly, openly, with passion, respect and romantic commitment. You may now be thinking, "That sounds interesting, but how does it work? How do people manage multiple partners? Just how do people organize time and space around sharing love with more than one person?"

My dear friend Ken responds that "Poly relationships are designer relationships. Each one is unique!" Another poly friend says, "There are as many ways of doing poly as there are poly people." They are both absolutely right. Neither answer, however, gives a poly newbie or curious onlooker a very clear picture of what poly looks like.

In the first chapter, I shared my personal history and how I discovered the word *polyamory*. Unfortunately, once I discovered the word, I had a precise picture of poly in my mind. It was what I'd been fantasizing about and working toward for my entire adult life. Back when I was first married and everyone was reading *Stranger in a Strange Land,* communes were sprouting like daffodils in spring, and lots of us were running around looking for a group to "grok" with. (I defined "grok" in the previous chapter.) My husband may have died, but the dream he and I shared was still alive and well in my heart.

My picture of polyamory was the child of that heady, revolutionary era. My friends jokingly called it "Mim's Think Tank and Swat Team." My dream was of five or maybe seven loving people living in a big round house where each person had a small private space linked to the inner common living room, kitchen, library and music room. We were infinitely diverse, in race, gender and sexual orientation as well as in the areas of skill and expertise we brought into the family. Sex was not the focus of the group, but was a glue that helped hold us together as we worked toward social change. Together, we'd learn and love and brainstorm great plans, then go out individually or in twos or threes as consultants to help schools, businesses, and other groups achieve positive change. New members were added by consensus, and we were a big loving family. That was what polyamory looked like, and I was thrilled to find a word for it so I could reach out and find others who wanted the same thing I wanted!

Then I actually met some poly people, and fell in love with a couple who also knew exactly what poly looked like, and it wasn't my hippie commune! But their vision included social activism, so I thought we could make a relationship work. The other two people in my newly formed Triad were flexible enough to agree that we could look for a few more than three, and I thought I was on my way to achieving my dream of that social activism think tank. But, as I shared in Chapter 1, distance and other things caused the Triad to end, so I was searching again.

At a poly conference in California, I met a charming polyamorous man who fell in love with me, despite the geographic distances between us at the time. He also knew exactly what poly looked like. We both said our vision of poly was not a great sea of different lovers, but a small, intimate family. Wow, I'd finally found a wonderful poly man whose dreams matched mine. We were made for each other! Life was good. That is, until I discovered that his fantasy of the perfect poly family was him and two hot bi babes who would live with him on his sailboat and be sister galley slaves. There would be no debate or conflict, because they would love and obey their wonderful Master, and together they'd sail the world in euphoric bliss. Think tanks and social activism weren't any more a part of his vision of polyamory than galley slaves were of

16

mine, yet we were both totally poly. And we loved each other and wanted to make a relationship work.

That was what first inspired me to start roughing out this book. In doing relationship coaching with a wide variety of couples across the country, I'm starting to hypothesize that the difference between the dreams and goals of two people with different visions of polyamory can be just as far apart as the difference between two people whose dreams are of monogamy and of polyamory. Not only are the goals diverse, but the partnership agreements, the commitments, and the social etiquette related to things such as how a new person is brought into relationship all vary with the type of poly relationship we fantasize about building. Yet I've seen lots of people who, like my sailor love and me, drift into poly relationships thinking that just because they say, "I'm poly," they share the same dream.

Let me be vulnerable and share some examples from my own experience with my wonderful poly sailor man. He has generously given me his permission, of course. All was love, bliss and fantasy, that is, until we started forming our poly family. I flew to Mexico to spend my birthday with him, and discovered that my birthday surprise was the fact that he'd just met a sexy new woman and had invited her to spend my birthday weekend on the boat with us. "What do you mean, you had no say in it?" he asked. "Why should that matter? We're poly, and we're totally open to new loves, and I know you're gonna love her. She likes sailing, she's open to poly, and I decided this would be a great way to celebrate your birthday."

So I beat myself up for not being thrilled. After all, I'm poly, and poly folks are always comfortable with other partners, right? I spent a lot of that vacation down the beach by myself, reading and talking to seagulls, so my sexy sailor and his hot new babe could have the boat to themselves.

In my vision of polyamory, and my experience with my husband, we met possible new partners, discussed them together, jointly invited them to dinner or something, and if we both decided we wanted to pursue the friendship, we did. And if it became sexual, it was because we all had discussed it first and decided that was a direction we all wanted to go. There were no surprises, and no unilateral decisions, even if they were disguised as birthday gifts. And we generally made love together, in the same room, even if for a while we paired off with the other people. There was never any need for me to disappear, in my version of poly. This sudden introduction to my love's vision of poly was tough for me. But my partner was as happy as a clam at high tide. He had his two babes on his sailboat, but this one wasn't being very submissive to the scene he'd created for us!

When I got back to my new home in New Mexico, I started finding people who shared my political passions, organized a discussion group to get acquainted with some of them, and when my sailor arrived, he thought it was all pretty boring. "But you're not even sleeping with any of them! How can these political discussion groups meet your needs, or lead to poly family?" We soon discovered that the differences between his and my fantasies of poly were almost as different as poly is from mono.

It was tough at first, because there are all kinds of ways of doing things that were different from what I was used to under my version of poly, in which potential new loves were introduced to existing loves and the decision to invite them into greater intimacy was a joint decision. That seemed like a totally cumbersome concept to my sailor man, who had no great desire to meet potential new loves of mine, and certainly didn't want his freedom limited by my desire to have input into loves he might choose. But we started realizing that dreams aren't set in concrete, and we cared for each other enough to openly discuss what needs each of us were hoping to meet through our quest for poly family, and how we could support each other in meeting separate needs while still developing the love we share. We realized that there wasn't a "right way" or a "wrong way" to do poly, but definitely different ways!

As I looked beyond my own relationship and started surveying the wide diversity within the poly movement, it started to look as if the only thing polys had in common was that they were *not* monogamous and they *were* honest and communicative. Yes, there may be as many ways of doing poly as there are poly people, and I realized how naïve I'd been when I thought finding poly meant finding people who were also looking for groups to "grok" with! But as I got to know more people and to see the types of relationships they had formed, some patterns started to emerge. I realized that if we became aware of the rich diversity within poly and had a vocabulary to describe the types of poly relationship models that we wanted, we would more readily be able to communicate our dreams to potential new partners, and to ourselves.

A caveat before we explore further: just as every monogamous relationship is unique yet it's helpful to have a word to describe the general style of relationship known as "monogamy," so is each poly relationship unique, yet it can be useful to have generic terms to describe types of relationships within polyamory. The general patterns I describe in this book are not presented as a way of putting people or relationships into boxes with labels firmly attached. Rather, the goal is to help us examine our own desires and find a vocabulary that enables us to more easily describe our relationship goals.

A second caveat is that nothing is forever, especially not dreams and fantasies. Dreams, fantasies, desires, and the relationships that result from them are never set in stone. They change as we grow and change. What we want when we're twenty-five may be quite different from what we want at fifty. Just as a relationship that starts out as monogamous may morph into a poly relationship, one form of a poly family may morph into a different one as it and the partners within it grow and change. The patterns described in this book are not cookie cutter molds, but simply my glimpse of general trends within our ever-changing community.

Since I'm a visual person, I've chosen the letters in the word POLYS to help describe five of the more common relationship formats that I've observed in the poly world. If one or more of the models resonate with you and describe the format of your relationship, I'd love to hear from you, perhaps with a brief description of your current family. I would love to have stories from poly families to use as anonymous "case examples" of various relationship models to share with others who are in the process of creating their own poly family.

So onward to discovering ways of describing some of the polydiversity within polyamorous partnership patterns!

Chapter 3

P: Plural Poly Pairs

Plump Poly Porcupines

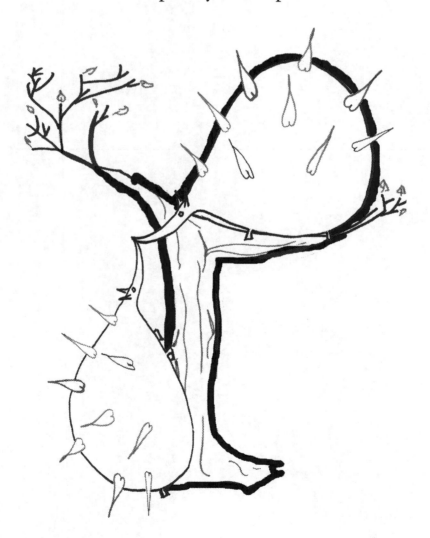

P: Plural Poly Pairs
Plump Poly Porcupines

"Love and marriage, love and marriage, go together like a horse and carriage," or so the old song tells us. Marriage between one man and one woman is held up as the bedrock of American civilization, at least by some of our conservative political and religious leaders. That is the family model in which most of us were raised, the model we saw all around us, the one that was held up as the ideal. Although many children grow up in single-parent families, that is often looked at as sub-optimal (and not only by the single parent having to do all the work!) Pairs are the accepted format of romantic love, virtually the only model we see in textbooks, the media and literature.

Some claim that humans are hard-wired to be pair-bonded. Whether it's biological wiring or societal conditioning, pair relationships are indisputably the most common form of romantic and sexual connection, not only in the heterosexual and the gay world but also among folks who identify as polyamorous.

Many of us who were around back in 1972 read what was considered a radical new book by Nena and George O'Neill, *Open Marriage*. Some still consider this book the "bible" of the swinger community, and it's good reading for all of us pursuing non-monogamous relationship styles, if only for its historical value. It laid the groundwork for a new model of marriage, one that was honest about choosing to be non-monogamous.

The Plural Poly Pairs relationship format tends to look a lot like the good old 70's style "open marriage." In the prototype of this relationship style, the central players are a committed pair, often actually married to each other (if they are heterosexual or lucky enough to live in one of the few places where committed couples of any gender are legally able to marry). Other Plural Poly Pairs are not married, but in a relationship which they consider primary, quite often living together.

What differentiates Poly Pairs from traditional couples, however, is their commitment to each other's freedom to pursue other pair relationships honestly and with the full support of their primary partner. The degree of freedom and what information about the outside partnerships is shared with the primary partner varies with each couple, and is ideally negotiated well before outside partnerships are formed, although in real life, all too often partners stumble into outside romances and then come home and start the work of negotiating ways of dealing with it. This after-the-fact negotiation can cause a lot of stress, not unlike the trauma of monogamous affairs. So, if you're in a basically monogamous relationship and contemplating working toward polyamory, please put some effort into thinking seriously about what you wish for. Start discussing it now, before acting on it in any way. It's a lot easier to stay calm and loving as you share fantasies and possibilities for your relationship while the ideas and fantasies are no more than that—just ideas and fantasies—rather than waiting until you're embroiled in the emotional turmoil of an actual outside romance.

You know the old saying, "Don't wait to study navigation until you're in the middle of a storm." Likewise, don't wait to negotiate an open marriage until you're in the heat of passion with an outside new love. One goal of this book is to discuss and describe relationship options, so couples can work out a navigation plan well in advance of leaving the comfortable harbor of monogamy. Many couples draw up a solid, written agreement before they head into the sometimes stormy seas of non-monogamous behavior. These agreements vary from family to family. There is no "right" or "wrong" agreement or contract, as long as it results from honest, non-coercive negotiation and meets the needs of both partners.

What does a good Poly Pair agreement include? For starters, all types of agreements for non-monogamous relationships must include solid, specific commitments regarding safer sex, and any lapses from following these agreements are serious threats to not only the physical, but also the emotional health of the primary relationship. They are absolute potential deal-breakers, so the safer sex agreements must be so specific that there are absolutely *no* areas for potential misunderstandings. Learning a potential new partner's sexual history is a vital first step, but by itself is not sufficient. "She said she hadn't had sex for a long time, so I figured that made it safe to not use a condom," is a recipe for disaster. Leave nothing to be decided in the heat of passion. Most poly agreements are based on consistent use of condoms, no matter how safe the sexual history sounds. Some agreements include the use of barriers for oral sex as well, and may extend to barriers for digital play, using gloves for sexual play with fingers and hands. Whatever the agreement, trust and safety depend on its being followed faithfully.

No move to becoming fluid-bonded with an outside partner (i.e., sex without condoms, thus exchanging body fluids) should be taken without a full discussion with the primary partner. Some couples feel that fluid-bonding should be based on more than the written medical test result and the appropriate waiting period necessary to indicate physical safety. They look at fluid-bonding as a symbol of an increased emotional bond, as well. (See the example of a fluid-bonding ceremony in the final chapter of this book.) Partners need to consider carefully what their own values and boundaries are, realizing that agreements are not written in stone and may be revised as needed, but only with the full consent of all partners.

Beyond the safer sex issues, agreements need to also address the social and emotional conditions that will make both primary partners, as well as their secondary lovers, feel valued, respected and secure. Will you discuss a potential new love with your partner? If so, when? Some couples agree to discuss a potential new person with their primary partner as soon as they feel the first spark of interest, well before any sexual contact takes place. Some partners want to meet the potential new love before any intimacy takes place. Others trust each other to go much further with a potential new love, simply asking that they be informed as soon as it is convenient.

Especially in early stages of a migration from monogamy to pair poly, some partners insist on what is often called "veto power," i.e., if I don't feel positive about him/her, I am free to tell you so, and if I don't like the person, you end the courtship immediately. At the other extreme, there are couples who find some variation of "Don't ask, don't tell" to be more comfortable. Only you and your partner can look within yourselves and investigate what is going to work for you. And what works today may no longer work, or no longer be needed, a month from now, in which case the "veto power" may be lifted, or the "don't ask, don't tell" modified to "just tell me what I ask," or even "Wow, I find hearing every juicy detail a real turn on, so please tell me all about your time together!"

Then there are the issues of time. Some pairs negotiate specific "free nights" when outside activities take place on a regular basis, whether they be simply "nights out with the boys" or dates with potential new loves. Others simply check with primary partners as opportunities arise. Many primary partners who do not want veto power over the *who* of outside relationship do want veto power over the *when*. Generally, the primary partner gets first dibs on special days, and has first choice on their partner's free time. Needless to say, emergencies trump casual dates, but primary partners need to be honest in not creating quasi-emergencies whenever their partner has dates planned.

Finances can be another challenge, especially if the primary partners pool their finances. "So you're taking her out Tuesday night," one partner might say, "but you're *not* gonna take money from our joint account to treat her to flowers and chocolates and dinner at the most expensive restaurant in town, one you and I haven't gone to for years." Most Poly Pairs find that having their own accounts, separate from the pooled family account, and funding outside dates from these private funds is a good way of avoiding conflict.

Many couples decide to keep certain activities exclusive within their primary relationship. These can vary from specific sexual activities to favorite restaurants, social activities or camping places that they want to reserve as private shared spaces.

Ways of dealing with the reconnection time with a primary partner after coming home from a date is another important issue, but it will be discussed a bit later in the section on poly etiquette in the various types of polyamorous relationships.

So once these agreements have been negotiated, what will a Plural Poly Pair relationship eventually look like? That, too, depends on the two of you, but in general, it will look like a pair of romantic Porcupines, nose to nose, each Porcupine having some additional pair relationships, like the quills of a Porcupine, each independent from each other and from their partner Porcupine.

Let's say Alec and Zia are a primary pair, nose to nose with solidly negotiated agreements in place. Alec decides to develop a relationship with Bailey, creating an Alec-Bailey partnership quill. Before long, he meets Cameron and forms an Alec-Cameron pair relationship. He eventually adds an Alec-Drew relationship, and possibly more if he has the time and interest. Zia knows about Bailey, Cameron and Drew, and all three secondary partners know about each other, or at least know that Alec has other relationships in addition to his primary bond with Zia. But the secondaries may never meet and may not know much about each other. What Zia knows about Alec's other lovers depends on the guidelines they have worked out in their agreement contract.

Similarly, Zia may eventually become intimate with Toni, Terry, and Taylor. Each of his relationships, like those of Alec, are pair relationships. The secondary partners are attached to one or the other of the primary partners like quills to a porcupine. Some partnership quills may be shed over time, and new ones may develop to take their place.

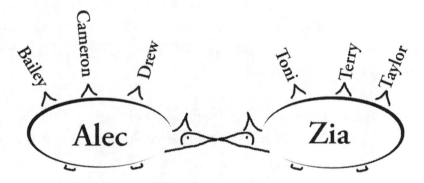

Poly-P Porcupine Plural Poly Pairs

Although honesty and respect are givens, as in all poly relationships, there is no necessity for Alec to get to know any of Zia's secondary lovers terribly well. Similarly, it is not likely that intimate friendships will develop between Zia and Alec's loves, or among the various secondary partners themselves. Each relationship is an intimate pair unto itself, not hidden, but intrinsically a private twosome.

Some Porcupine Pair Partners agree to share with each other the basic details of their secondary relationships. Others decide that what happens within each pair partnership is confidential and of no particular interest to their other partners. Sure, Alec and Zia might happen to be at the same social event as Bailey, Cameron, Terry or Toni, and since the entire relationship cluster is based on honesty and openness, hopefully everyone will be comfortable and friendly. But the focus is not on getting them all together, let alone jumping into the same bed together. Rather, Porcupine Pairs function by scheduling private time for each of the various intimate pairs.

Incidentally, Plural Pair Poly is an ideal form for mono-poly couples where one person wants secondary partners while the other is supportive of their partner's polyamorous lifestyle but does not want outside lovers of their own. Sometimes the monogamous partner wants to know their poly partner's lovers on a friendship basis, or they may not desire any involvement with the outside loves.

Some people say that a single poly person is, by definition, a Poly Porcupine. However, I do not see it that way. I've always tended to define polyamory not by what one is doing at a particular time, but by the person's ultimate goal, fantasy, or desire. During the time I lived in rural Alaska, not a happy hunting ground for relationships of any type, let alone poly ones, I had a magnet on my fridge that said, "I'm just two people short of a ménage à trois !" I'll loan it to any of you singles out there whose fantasy is a Triad!

A single poly may look to outsiders like a Porcupine, with one or more pair relationships surrounding them. But a closer look will tell more. If a single poly person works to facilitate friendships and social activities among the various people they go out with, it may indicate that they're working toward the eventual goal of forming one of the more inclusive forms of poly. If they keep each relationship separate, sharing only that they have other relationships but not much about them, then they're hinting that the Porcupine model is, at the moment, their choice.

Benefits of the Poly-P Plural Pairs Model

The greatest benefits of the Plural Poly Pair model are the personal freedom it gives each of the primary partners, the ease of forming new pair relationships, and the fact that all Poly-P interactions are based on the comfortable, familiar model of pair courtship rituals.

Perhaps the latter is the most powerful. Most people have had some practice in the traditional ritual of "boy notices girl, girl smiles, boy asks girl out," etc. Pairs are familiar; we know how to behave in a pair relationship. We know how to make love to one person, and aren't quite sure what would go where if there were three in the bed, let alone how to relax into a threesome without worrying about whether we're giving each partner equal attention and pleasure. Pairs just feel natural to most people, because we've been there, done that!

Freedom is the second great advantage of this form of poly. Girl sees boy, finds him attractive, starts a conversation, and where it goes from there is only limited by the terms of the agreement she has chosen to negotiate with her primary partner. Perhaps she calls home and tells him she's not going to be home tonight. If they've negotiated a "tell me first" clause, she'll tell him she's going out on a date with a new guy. Unless their contract includes veto power, she's totally free to make all her own decisions, so long as she follows their safer sex rules. She does not have to consider whether or not the new guy will fit into their family preferences, or whether he shares any of her primary's interests and values. Actually, she's probably looking for someone who meets some needs her primary doesn't meet. If her primary partner likes opera but she hates opera and loves Country Western, she's thrilled that new guy has Dwight Yoakam playing in his truck. He suggests they go for Mexican food. Good thing they're not all three going to dinner, since her partner hates Mexican! She's free as a bird to form relationships that are just for her, not potential additions to a family.

The ease of forming new relationships is a direct result of the personal freedom in the Poly-P model. The primary pair has already discussed how much or how little they want to know about each other's outside relationships, and they play no role whatsoever in choosing their partner's other pair relationships, with the possible exception of using their veto power if they've negotiated that. (Only a relatively small percentage of Porcupine Pairs choose to have veto power, and those who start out with veto rights often delete it from their agreement once they become more comfortable with their partner's track record of choosing partners.) So forming a new relationship is only slightly more difficult for a Porcupine than it is for a single person. Well, that's not quite true. A good Porcupine will choose to tell a potential new partner about their poly primary fairly early in the new relationship, and if the potential partner is really looking for a monogamous relationship—searching for Mr/Ms Marriage Material—they may exit the scene. But once that hurdle has been crossed, the new pair can make dates, do things together as often as they can fit time together into their schedules, and develop their own unique partnership without any intrusion from the other relationship(s) that either has developed.

Challenges of the Poly-P Plural Pairs Model

One pillar in the poly belief system is that love is not a limited resource; there is plenty of it to share freely. However, time *is* a limited resource; we each get just 24 hours of it per day, only seven days per week. No matter how strongly we are convinced that the love we give to other partners does not in any way affect the love we have for our primary partner, the fact of the matter is that the *time* Alec schedules with Bailey, Cameron and Drew does take away from the time spent with Zia. This causes no problems if Zia is also scheduling time with Taylor, Terry and Toni, if he has an exciting job that demands more time than Alec's work does, or if Zia really enjoys having some time at home alone, just to relax and have the house to himself. However, maintaining a time-need balance can become a challenge, especially if one partner has a wealth of outside partners to schedule time with and the other has none at the moment and is squealing "Wee, wee, wee, I want some!"—some more of your time, some more of your attention, or maybe more lovers of my own, and they just haven't materialized!

The ease of forming new partnerships because no input from the primary is necessary has a flip side. It can leave a primary partner feeling disconnected from major parts of their partner's life. The fewer details that the primary partners contract to share about other relationships, the greater the potential for disconnection. It is vital to review the agreement regularly, a minimum of once a year, and to be open to frequent revisions. Perhaps Alec initially thought he didn't want to know any details of Zia's romances, then finds that his fears and fantasies of what is happening between Zia and Toni are way wilder than the juiciest reality could be! While Alec is busy trying to be comfortable with this wild, hot romance that, in his imagination, Zia is having with his outside loves, Zia may find that he really longs to share with his beloved Alec some of the trouble he's running into with other loves, but feels unable to bring up the subject because Alec had said he didn't want to know anything about them. Realizing that all agreements are continual works in process enables Alec and Zia to reopen the issue and share their feelings with each other. They may or may not decide to renegotiate, but communication about their agreements needs to stay open to prevent the development of toxic levels of disconnection.

Another danger to Plural Pair Poly relationships is also the flip side of a benefit. Pairs are comfortable, familiar and cozy. Due to the freedom in forming them and the confidentiality that may exist within each pair, an outside partner can start to believe that their pair bond will eventually become more intense than the bond between the two primary partners. In some of the other poly models, the various lovers often do things together, so Bailey has the opportunity to witness the strength and juiciness of Alec and Zia's relationship. However, when Porcupine Alec is with Bailey, theirs is the only relationship Bailey experiences first-hand, so she can build unrealistic expectations for its future, despite the honesty with which Alec has informed Bailey of his relationship with Zia. Over the years, I've noticed a fair number of lonely singles fishing in the poly pond, consciously or unconsciously figuring that sharing a love is better than not having any love at all. Unfortunately, once they find a partner, their mono goals surface and they start hoping that this wonderful relationship they've finally found will become so hot that their poly partner's other relationships, including the primary one, will simply melt away. Once in a while this actually does happen, but it usually doesn't work for long, and the result tends to include more drama than any of us really want!

Another challenge is the temptation to chop ones time and romantic life into too many pieces, thus settling for a rather shallow level of commitment with each partner. Instead of working to expand and grow within a relationship, Poly Porcupines can simply turn to different partners to fulfill different needs, keeping each partnership from growing into all it could be. I've seen Poly-P partnerships that looked a bit like "if this is Tuesday, it must be Drew!" Partners can close their eyes to conflict by filling their lives with alternative lovers, rather than working out relationship issues with their primary partner.

Another problem with Plural Poly Pairs can be caused by the absence of interaction between a person's various partners. This can mean that a primary partner misses out on the input, love, juiciness and depth of texture that is one of the joys of multi-partner relationships in which each partner enhances the life of all the others involved and adds to the wealth and depth of the total shared community relationship. Simplicity and ease of formation come at the cost of depth and diversity of experience, communication, and insight.

A word should also be said about the danger of triangulation, relationship discussions which exclude key members, and this will be discussed in the section about poly etiquette.

Despite these hazards, the Plural Pair model is one of the most prevalent forms of poly. It is also the starting point in the vast majority of poly relationships, as will be discussed in the section on "morphing to other forms."

Most effective ways of introducing new members

The great joy of the Poly Pair model is that, under some agreements, new members don't need to be introduced at all! I know Poly-P couples whose secondary partners have never so much as talked with their lover's primary, let alone met them. However, at least in fairly long-term secondary relationships, this tends to be the exception rather than the rule. It isn't much fun to be a secondary who can't even call the home of a lover for fear of the primary answering the phone. In most relationships, since everyone at least knows about the existence of other partners, a certain level of comfort with casual telephone or social encounters is the norm.

Since it is likely that partners will eventually run into each other, some poly folks develop an etiquette or policy of initiating at least minimal communication between the primary partner and potential new loves. I've developed my own personal habit for dealing with people who are in Poly Pair relationships. When a potential new lover expresses an interest in me, saying that his primary partner is totally comfortable with him taking new partners, I say, "I trust you and am sure your primary is okay with you and me becoming intimate. So just to make things more smooth, I'd really like to meet her first, to give her the chance to tell me herself that she welcomes my entering into a relationship with you."

If the guy flees with his tail between his legs, I know that "it ain't necessarily so" and that I've avoided getting into a relationship fraught with some degree of dishonesty, which can lead to unwanted drama, and does not meet my standard of poly honesty.

Unfortunately, this totally open way of starting a relationship with a new partner does not seem to be terribly common. I have yet to have one of my primary partner's potential loves make any effort to communicate with me. To be honest, this hurts. But I try to be content with my primary's reticence to suggest to potential new loves that they make contact with me. So our current agreement is based on our right to do things differently from each other. I respect his desire to start relationships that are not preceded by any contact with me, and he respects my desire to make contact with the primary of any potential lover, and to introduce him to that potential love as well. See how much flexibility there can be in poly agreements, not only between those of two different families, but also between the members within one family?

So to summarize, the effective way of introducing new members within Plural Pair Poly relationships is simply to follow the guidelines you have agreed upon. And when things just aren't working, take a look at your agreement. Maybe one or the other of you, or both, are starting to long for a gradual morph into a less independent form of poly.

Since all relationships start with individuals, and since, as mentioned above, poly singles tend to look like Poly Porcupines, this is a good place to include a little about the most effective ways for a single person to look for potential poly partners. The first step singles need to deal with is letting new dates know, right from the beginning, that a monogamous marriage is not what they are looking for. That scares a lot of potential lovers away, but it saves a lot of drama on down the road.

This challenge is largely avoided by looking for partners at poly gatherings or websites. Poly Matchmaker (www.polymatchmaker.com), the Loving More website (www.lovemore.com), and other sites focusing on non-monogamous relationships are good places to start. Even better, find a local poly group, and make plans to go to a national or regional conference of Loving More, Poly Living, or some other poly organization. These same suggestions can apply to Poly Porcupines looking for a few new quills.

Agreement issues for Poly-P Plural Pairs

The issues Poly Porcupines need to negotiate are similar to those in all poly relationships, with a focus on deciding how much input and information each partner wants about other partnerships, and when they want this information and/or input. A Poly-P agreement might include:

Vision of our relationship:
    Our picture of what this model looks like for us
    Degree of personal freedom each of us desires
    Things that we choose to keep exclusive within our primary relationship
    Degree of relationship confidentiality desired within secondary partnerships
    How we are to show interest and/or support for our partner's secondary relationships
    How we can be help each other when secondary relationships cause stress

Safer Sex Agreements:
    Concrete agreements about the use of barriers
    What will be shared about the sex history and other sexual aspects of the new partner
    What, when, and how secondary loves might be admitted to fluid-bonded status

Information:
    When to inform our primary partner about potential, emerging, or actualized
        relationships
    What and how much to tell partner about secondary lovers
    What and how much to share about dates, sexual and other activities with secondary
    What and how much to share about issues, joys, and challenges in the outside
        relationship
    What and how much about primary relationship should be shared with outside
        partner(s)

Input:
    When, how, and whether a new partner is to be introduced to primary
    Degree of input requested from primary, i.e., none; opinions; advice; veto power
    What input primary may share about the progress of secondary relationships
    What, how, and how much to share about outside relationships when they end
    Degree and type of input regarding scheduling times for dates

Changes:
    How to request changes in behavior regarding secondary relationships
    How to request that the agreement be reopened to discuss possible revisions
    How often agreement will be automatically scheduled for a review
    Techniques for joint decision making and conflict resolution

Poly etiquette for Poly-P Porcupines

Etiquette within the Poly-P model may be easier than in any other model, yet behavior in this relationship model is possibly the most fraught with the possibility for creating hurt and distance if sensitive etiquette guidelines are not followed.

Negotiating communication commitments in advance is vital, as is acting on them consistently. Partners must also share when they're feeling a need to renegotiate their agreements, as relationships do grow and change. Since there is often minimal interaction between primaries and their partner's secondary(s), many people assume that there will be fewer communication issues in Poly-P relationships than in more inclusive forms of poly. But no matter what level of communication is agreed upon, life happens, and chance encounters can cause discomfort if one has not prepared oneself to deal with them. Conventional etiquette of the monogamous world gives us little help in this arena. The media provide no models other than totally non-poly reactions like, "I'm gonna scratch their eyes out; get out the butcher knife; blow them away with my 7mm Magnum!"

Some simple guidelines can help make meeting an outside partner of one's primary partner more comfortable, whether the meet-up be planned or a chance encounter. The first rule of etiquette in any interchange is normal politeness, accompanied by deep breaths to be sure the fight-flight impulse doesn't take over! Ideally, a secondary will show respect for the status of the primary partner, perhaps expressing appreciation for the primary's willingness to share the valuable time and affection of their magnificent mate.

However, dear primaries, don't hold your breath and wait for this to happen, as a secondary may be too nonplussed to know what to say or do. Remember, no matter how well your primary partner has described your supportive poly stance, the secondary is still faced with the traditional culture's derogatory view of "the other woman/man." So if the secondary does not genuflect and offer to kiss your ring, be the gracious Queen Bee that you are and tell the secondary how happy you are for the joy he is bringing to your beloved, or how flexible she is about the limited time she gets to have with your partner, or something else that you can say with honesty and grace. Since chance encounters are bound to happen sooner or later, it is my strong recommendation that, if necessary, you practice these polite statements in the mirror…

and keep practicing until they actually come from an honest place of good poly compersion! (Review the end of the first chapter to refresh yourself on the definition of compersion.)

Agreeing with, or respecting different preferences, regarding contact between primaries and new loves is critical to a Poly Porcupine's success. This issue was addressed in the section on bringing new people into a relationship. It is my opinion that, if contact is to be made, it is more polite when the request comes from the potential new person. Their effort to contact the primary partner is not only a way of showing respect for the primary partnership, but also helps open positive communication lines. If a new partner contacts a primary, it is obviously the role of the primary to thank the new partner for their openness, and to express, as honestly as possible, support and joy in seeing the new relationship evolve.

If a partner chooses to arrange a meeting between her primary and her new love, it is her responsibility to facilitate open communication and try to make them both comfortable. Needless to say, it is not helpful to let the conversation become a duet between her and new love about the great party they just went to, all that happened at it, and stories about the other people there, none of whom her primary knows, thus leaving her primary love shut out of the conversation loop! You may laugh, but I've experienced exactly that, and it isn't fun. Focusing on what your two lovers have in common and helping them get to know each other will facilitate trust and comfort, which is the goal of the meeting. If new love is new to poly, a little prompting before the meeting about how to show respect for the primary might be helpful.

Needless to say, triangulation in poly relationships is never good etiquette, nor does it add to the health of the relationship. Triangulation is any discussion of group dynamics or interpersonal issues that takes place without the knowledge and input of a key member, especially if this is the member being discussed. For example, it's not a good idea for a secondary to call the primary to discuss the wonderful or less-than-wonderful qualities of the lover they share! It can be death to a relationship if the primary uses the secondary relationship to whine about all that is wrong with the primary relationship, or vice versa. How can a challenge be resolved if key players are excluded from its discussion, and may not even know it exists? A firm rule against two partners talking about another behind the latter's back is essential. Unfortunately, it's a common trap even well-meaning people fall into. It can destroy a loving relationship and totally undermine trust. So avoiding triangulation is a lot more than just polite etiquette.

Now we come to a biggie: etiquette for returning home to the primary after a date with a secondary. This can be the best part of being poly—or the worst! Like most matters of etiquette, the goal is to avoid hurt and drama while nurturing love, comfort and positive feelings. Again, conventional etiquette has probably gotten us through the date with the new secondary just fine, focusing on eye contact, little niceties like perhaps presenting her with a flower or two, complimenting him on how handsome he looks, listening attentively and asking appropriate questions, not hogging the air time, etc. But conventional etiquette doesn't give us any equally useful tips for how to come home to main love after a hot date!

A poly friend of mine puts it this way: whatever you do to court a new potential love, do the same in spades to court your existing love! If you took the new love a rose, come home to your partner with a gift of three roses. If you took your new love to Pizza Hut (god forbid) invite your primary love out for steak. All too often, especially among partners taking their first tentative steps into non-monogamy, shiny new love object is so exciting that comfortable secure lover gets overlooked, or treated like an overstuffed chair, which is *not* the way to create a happy, long-lasting poly relationship!

If your agreement includes sharing about the other person and/or what you did, do it with honesty and enthusiasm, but avoid comparisons. Needless to say, pay close attention to the "hot buttons" or insecure areas that experience has taught you that your primary has. If she has always worried about her tiny breasts, you'll be wise not to start the description of potential new love with "She was wearing this low-cut blouse that really showed off those two gorgeous heavers of hers!" If he is uptight about size (and how many American men aren't?) don't start off your description of your first hot sex together with anything like "I've wanted to feel totally filled that way for soooooooo long!" Statements like, "I loved running my hand through her long, thick hair" can be merely an honest description to one person, but a real ouch to a woman with short, thinning hair. I think you get the picture. Be honest, but not to the point of creating a picture of perfection contrasted with that huge list of inadequacies that may belong to your home partner.

The other extreme, "She sure doesn't know how to give blow jobs like yours," although not as immediately hurtful, can also breed competitiveness. Instead, statements like "I love you so much, and love you even more for your courage in being open to sharing me!" focus on what is intrinsically good about your relationship with your primary. You might try, "It was lots of fun, and the entire time I was with him, I found myself thinking about how much I desire you, my love, how much you mean to me, and how lucky I am to have a beautiful partner who is confident enough of our relationship to share me like this." These types of statements, if totally honest, are positive ways of assuring your partner that replacement is not on the agenda. And if you're really poly, you'll find that the statement really is true. I've never been with a secondary partner for any length of time without my primary being in my mind and heart, too. That's what makes poly so much fun.

Many polys say that this re-courting after a date leads to the hottest sex they've had in a while. That's another fringe benefit of poly. And if your primary knows that he's gonna get an extra dose of your attention and affection right after you have a date with someone else, he'll be more open to your next outside date!

Asking your primary how she was feeling while you were gone is another way of saying, "You are the most important part of all this, and I really care about what this is like for you, not just for me." Whatever your partner says, your role is to listen and absorb what is shared, no matter what it is, holding your partner in your arms and thanking her for being so open and sharing. Needless to say, responses like "You shouldn't have felt that way," are too insensitive to even consider. If you find stuff like that coming out of your mouth, or your head, go back and review a good book on Active Listening!

All this is not only important after first dates with new partners, or for primaries first experimenting with non-monogamy. The need for positive homecoming habits becomes more important as time goes on. They're also vital if your relationship comes to the point of discussing morphing into some other, more inclusive form of polyamory. And the need to avoid comparison extends to the home partner as well, not just the partner with the hot new love. It's hard to not worry and compare, especially when you're sitting home alone fantasizing about what your mate is doing with her sexy new lover. This is especially challenging in "don't ask, don't tell" forms of Poly-P where the only thing one has is one's imagination. Many couples make a habit of not staying home alone when their partner has a date. An exciting movie with a friend is a better way to spend the evening.

A poly love of mine who has a 32-year successful marriage uses a term I like. He calls his special times with his primary "tending my garden." This aptly describes the core of poly etiquette: while exploring new terrain, never forget or overlook the joy of tending that beautiful garden at home!

Morphing to Poly-P from other forms of poly and to other models from it

As mentioned above, the Poly Pair model, basically an open marriage, is the most common way in which couples morph from monogamy to polyamory. Some monogamous couples first experiment with swinging, which is also a strongly pair-based form of non-monogamy. However, swinging is different from the Porcupine Pair Poly model in that in swinging, the primary couple often makes contacts with other couples, and many swingers only play with other couples, often in the presence of their primary partner. Porcupine Poly allows for more individual freedom, in that each partner is free to establish one-on-one relationships without the participation of their primary partner. Poly-P is also different from swinging in that each of the pair relationships is based on some degree of emotional connection between the two partners, rather than just on the fun of external sexuality.

Although the drawings on the cover give a sneak preview of each of the forms discussed in the book, it is difficult to talk about ways the Poly-P may morph into other poly formats before all of them have been fully described. Nevertheless, since relationships do not remain static, each chapter will end with a description of how that form often morphs into other forms. You can always look back over these sections after you've finished reading the full descriptions of each of the poly forms.

Many couples morph from Poly-P to other forms of polyamory, especially as the emotional contacts within pairs becomes strong enough that partners want a more open relationship that includes more than one partner. Sometimes the progression is from veto power or "don't ask, don't tell" to greater trust and sharing between primaries and secondary loves. Sometimes a secondary becomes a genuine friend of their lover's primary, and this friendship develops into a more egalitarian Poly-L (often called "V") relationship and eventually a Triad. Sometimes the entire group of loves morphs into an intimate network or Poly-Y, as secondary loves form additional loves of their own.

It is not as common for Paired Porcupines to morph into the group-focused Poly-O form of polyamory, although it has been known to happen. This is probably because the initial goal of many people in Poly Pair relationships is individual freedom, which is one of the greatest benefits of the Poly-P model. People whose dream is the Poly-O model tend to value group dynamics above individualism. Once outside partnerships have been formed, based on individual choice rather than group consensus, it is not terribly likely that these relationships will morph into a communal group "grok" type of relationship. But it has been known to happen, especially when the initial contract included a lot of sharing, and the couple has seen pair-choosing as a tentative first step into the brave new world of polyamory, with an eventual goal of finding and forming an extended family.

It is also possible that secondary loves eventually meet each other and form connections between themselves, which might, by chance, morph into The Poly-S Sensuous Chain. This, however, is a less likely option than morphing into a Poly-L Triad or Poly-Y network. Of course, many Porcupine Pairs have no intention of morphing into any other type of relationship format, and a vast majority of poly folks choose to remain in the Poly-P Plural Pairs model happily ever after.

Chapter 4

O: Old-Fashioned GROK

The Poly-O Family Circle

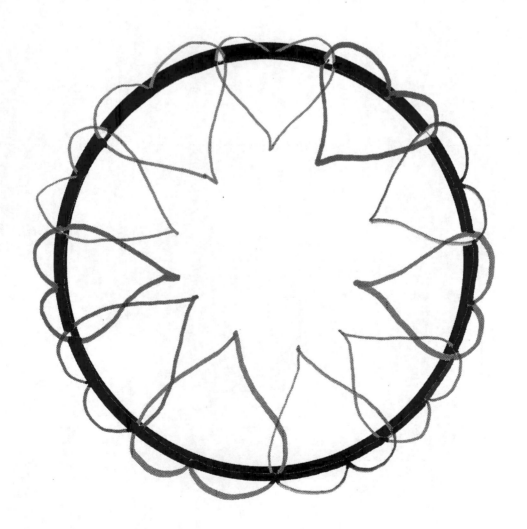

O: Old-fashioned GROK
The Poly-O Family Circle

Just as Poly Plural Pair Porcupines can look back at the O'Neill's *Open Marriage* as one source of their relationship style, many families with an O-shaped Poly Circle have found Heinlein's *Stranger in a Strange Land* a source of inspiration. This novel, an icon of the 60's and 70's era, coined the word *GROK* to represent love among a group of people, usually a group with mutual dedication to a cause or a shared vision of life. The reason why Heinlein created this new word was that he wanted a name for the different type of love he envisioned, neither the limited romantic love of traditional ownership-based marriages, nor a mere "group grope" or sexual orgy. Rather, *GROK* was an intellectual, spiritual, and emotional shared love, which might include sexuality, although sex was not the focus or primary purpose. The concept of *GROK* was one of the inspirations for the wide variety of intentional communities that sprang up during this heady, exciting era of massive social change. And it is a great description for the Poly-O Family.

In some ways, Poly-O is the opposite of the Poly-P model of polyamory. Just as independence and individual freedom are core values for a Poly-P, the value of belonging to a group in which everyone is equal and emotionally connected is a cornerstone of Poly-O Families. Therefore, it is no surprise that these two models may be the oldest forms of polyamory within the modern movement. They meet two different sets of needs. The other models described in this book are basically offshoots or derivations of these two basic forms.

A Poly-O might be thought of as a small intentional community. Often, it includes people of diverse ages, races, even sexual orientations. Ideally, each person has unique skills, which they bring into the family, to the benefit of all. Mary may love to cook, so she can be the primary chef of the family. Paul, a construction worker, may be the family builder and "fix-it" man. Sara, an educator, may be in charge of the children's homework, or may even provide home schooling. Gary may be the family gardener, while Kerri takes care of the finances, investments, and legal needs. The various members are linked together like a giant O. Just as the energy of the Poly Porcupine tends to be focused outward toward new pair partnerships, the energy of the Poly-O is focused inward, toward the shared community.

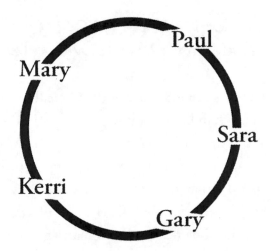

a Poly-O Family Circle

Both singles and people already in a partnership gravitate toward Poly-O relationships. However, once a part of the Poly-O Family, couples tend to morph into the group rather than maintaining the primary nature of their relationship to each other. Potential new members generally start as friends who are invited to join in the family dinners at times, and so gradually get to know the family and its members, while the family discusses whether or not the newcomer(s) would fit into the group. The goal in welcoming new members is that they will enhance the family as a whole, and that the family will enhance the life of each new member, so the addition will add something to the quality of life of everyone involved. Since most important decisions are made by group consensus, if one family member has strong negative feelings about a potential new member, it is not likely that this person will be invited to join the Poly-O Family.

This is a key factor that differentiates the Poly-O from the Poly-P. If my Poly-P primary partner meets someone he finds attractive, there is no need for me to also like the person. Unless we have chosen to give each other veto power, my partner simply goes on to build a relationship with the new love, as my dislike of the person is no reason for him to not pursue the new playmate. It's not my relationship, so it's not my concern. Needless to say, this makes finding new partners much easier for Poly-P's than for Poly-O's. Most Poly-O fans, however, say the trade off is greater long-term intimacy, harmony and joy.

As among Poly-P's, agreements are vital. Poly-O contracts tend to be longer, and to be revised rather often, as new family needs and desires arise. Like group houses or larger intentional communities, most Poly-O Families have regular dinners together during which some time is set aside to discuss individual concerns, family plans, group problems, or requests for revision of the contract. Like all polyamorous relationships, the Poly-O Family is egalitarian, so everyone has an equal voice in making group decisions. Family discussions may take only a few minutes during a weekly check-in time, or they may be full-scale investigations of the "state of the union," or anything in-between.

Some Poly-O Families are polyfidelitous, meaning that the group is sexually exclusive within itself, members having sex with a variety of others in the family, but not with people outside the group. This makes Poly-O Family members safe from STD worries, and also makes sexuality a sort of glue that holds the family together, just as it does in pair relationships, but with greater sexual and emotional variety built in. Other Poly-O Families are non-exclusive, agreeing that members can have outside lovers so long as they follow the group's contract for safer sex and other relationship issues. However, since those who choose a Poly-O model tend to be group oriented, their primary energy tends to go into the shared activities of the family. In return, the family meets their need for belonging, love, stimulation, sexual diversity, growth and security.

Sure, a small outside fling once in a while may scratch an itch, but outside relationships of any depth take time and energy away from the group, do not contribute to the major goal of collaborative community, and can sometimes actually become divisive. Things like "Who'll take my turn on dishes so I can go out with this cutie I just met at the coffee shop?" or "I know it's my night to sleep with you, Mary dear, but I'm afraid I won't be home tonight. Ta ta…" may work once in a while, but make a habit of it and your family may decide you need to migrate out and be your own little Porcupine self!

Poly-O Families share child rearing and work together on family chores, sharing or dividing up tasks based on individual interests and talents. Some Poly-O Families run a family farm or business, but more often individual members pursue their own careers and have their own personal finances, with everyone contributing to a group account to pay for the expenses of the home. Many Poly-O Families do not even share the same house, as large homes are not easy to find. They may live in separate homes and simply get together as often as possible. So individuals within Poly-O relationships generally have a fair share of independence, counterbalanced by the security provided by being a member of an intimate group.

One specifically child-focused type of Poly-O Family can emerge from the changes caused by a divorce. In one family I know, Ronnie and Rylee had been married for about ten years and had three children. As the relationship changed and encountered problems, the couple split up, with Ronnie moving to a house across town, and the children migrating between the two houses so the pair could continue to co-parent. Not only was maintaining two separate houses a major financial drain, but the children, already stressed by the family split, hated moving between two different homes, bedrooms and community playmates.

Eventually, the couple decided to move back into the same house, Rylee having the upstairs bedroom, Ronnie a downstairs room, and the kids maintaining their original rooms. Eventually Rylee fell in love with Rowan, then Ronnie met Robin, and before long, Rowan and Robin had moved in. Robin brought a child from a prior partnership and pretty soon they were all integral parts of the family and the child-rearing process, a win-win for everyone. The children all had playmates, Robin was no longer struggling with the challenges of being a single mom, and even Ronnie and Rylee discovered that they got along better now than before. Eventually another partner, Reese, joined the group, and the five adults and four children have moved to a slightly bigger house, thanks to the adults pooling their resources rather than maintaining their separate houses. The last I heard, another single father and his child had joined this Poly-O. With luck and good communication skills, they will live and love happily ever after.

A common small Poly-O that often evolves from pre-existing committed pairs is the Quad, a four-person family. Two couples may become good friends, do things together, possibly assist each other in child-rearing, and eventually develop attractions between mates. In the popular Peyton Place version of the story, divorces are imminent. In the poly version, they find a big old house, move in together, and become a big, happy poly family. Or, if they are not comfortable being "out" as poly, they maintain separate houses near each other, spend lots of time together, and take joint family vacations. The Poly-O Quad can be a very stable form of extended family, giving children two male and two female role models, and providing the adults with sexual and emotional variety while still looking like normal, monogamous couples. As a fringe benefit, a Quad gives each person a sister-wife or brother-husband, and provides the kids with more playmates.

Benefits of the Poly-O Family Circle Model

Some individuals are first drawn to Poly-O group living because of the financial benefits it provides. Many Poly-O Families live in a group house or on a shared plot of rural land, each individual having private space of their own while the group shares a large common kitchen and communal living area. The cost-effectiveness of this arrangement is obvious. Instead of each individual or couple having to own or rent and maintain a separate house, kitchen, guest room, exercise room, library, and child play area, the group can pool resources and provide a much larger shared area which they all enjoy, rather than the small areas each could afford on their own. This is environmentally beneficial as well as financially advantageous. In addition, the group shares the work, doing what they're best suited for and enjoy the most, thus providing more time for group fun and interaction, as well as a high degree of security and protection from loneliness.

Another reason why some individuals or pre-existing couples are attracted to the Poly-O model is because of children. As mentioned earlier, the isolated nuclear family does not work very well for many people, as evidenced by a sea of latch-key kids and an epidemic of family stress that all too often leads to divorce. Throughout history, and still in many cultures, children are raised by a group of loving adults—a tribe, clan, or extended family. I have met numerous Poly-O Families that were formed specifically so that children would have more loving adults to participate in their upbringing.

Creating a Poly-O can be a positive response to changes in existing marital relationships. When a couple finds that it is time for a change, if instead of breaking the family up, they manage to add partners to meet their individual needs, thus morphing into a Poly Circle, it gives the children stability in a time of family stress and provides them with more loving adults as parents and role-models. The extended family provides both children and adults with a much healthier environment as compared to the financial, emotional and social stresses that often come with single parenting. Needless to say, expanding a loving circle rather than moving into a house all alone is also beneficial to both of the partners of the initial relationship.

Another benefit of the Poly-O model is that it avoids the calendar and time stretching elements that are a bane in the existence of members of Poly-P relationships. One doesn't have to leave one's primary love several nights a week in order to schedule time with a variety of secondary partners. And there are no conflicts over which lover to spend holidays with, because the whole family spends Thanksgiving together!

One thing I personally like about group living is that, ironic as it might seem, it gives one more private time, while at the same time offering freedom from loneliness. In a pair relationship, if your partner wants to chat, you're the only one there, so you usually end up together talking. If you want time alone and your partner is lonely, compromise is necessary. In a group, when you want someone to be with (sexually or socially) you can go to the common area and there's sure to be someone there to be with. If you want time alone, you can go to your private area to read, meditate, or just relax with no sense of deserting a needy partner.

Seniors are a group of people who are starting to migrate to some variation of the Poly-O model. Their children are grown and gone, past partners may be divorced or deceased, and the prospect of growing old alone is not pleasant, either financially or socially. Our society's fixation on the youth culture often makes it difficult for seniors to find partners, leaving their needs and desires for ongoing sexual, social, intellectual and spiritual intimacy unfulfilled. As life expectancy increases, people can look forward to over half of their adult life taking place in their post-child-rearing years. Often sexual desire increases, especially for women now freed from worrying about children. Current 60-somethings came of age during the sexual revolution and may have actually lived in communes or group houses back then, so they are familiar with the concept of shared living and shared intimacy. Finding like-minded people, pooling funds, and starting a Poly-O group home can provide the security we need as we age, along with the sexual freedom and excitement we still crave, and which research has shown is vital to maintaining our physical, intellectual, and emotional health during our mature years.

Challenges of the Poly-O Family Circle Model

Communication is a prerequisite of any good relationship, mono or poly, but the need for solid communication skill increases exponentially with the number of people in a relationship. Swingers have been known to joke that polys are so busy communicating that we don't have time to get around to sex! It is true that in a swinger relationship, you can go to a party with your partner, find some new partners with whom to have sex, play for the evening, then leave with your partner. That does provide a higher ratio of sex to communication!

Not only is the *quantity* of communication in Poly-O Families higher, but the *quality* needs to be pretty high, too. Consensus decision-making is not easy, and it demands a lot of honesty, flexibility, and time. If you don't enjoy the process of group decision-making, Poly-O is not for you.

In the Poly-P chapter, we discussed what some people believe is a hard-wired human preference for pair bonding. People with a strong desire for pair relationships will find Poly-O a challenge. Issues of sexual or emotional possessiveness can play havoc within a Poly-O group. Over time, groups have experimented with a wide variety of techniques for dealing with this. They range from strict sexual schedules like those developed by the Kerista and other intentional communities in which each person sleeps with each other member once before spending a second night with any one person, to totally free-flowing sexuality which often includes group sex among some or all of the group's members. Full group sensuality is generally quite common, some Poly-O Families practicing nudity or naturism, others simply ending group meetings with group hugs or "puppy piles."

Without a doubt, for those poly folks (like me) who really enjoy group sex, this is the poly form that is most likely to provide it. However, sexuality is totally optional, and there are usually some people within the group who are not sexual with each other, although they share emotional intimacy. In many small Poly-O Families, a casual sex rotation routine has evolved simply to avoid "and where shall I sleep tonight?" issues. A Poly-O Quad may decide to just alternate bed-partners on alternate nights. Other families have a more spontaneous format in which members have their own private spaces that they share however and whenever they wish with as many or few partners as they please. But all this requires far more communication than within a Poly-P relationship where each person goes his or her own way without much impact on the other "quill" pairs.

Compersion was discussed in the introduction to polyamory. For people still struggling with huge loads of insecurity and jealousy, seeing and/or hearing one partner sharing wild, juicy joy with someone else in the family can be tough. On the other hand, for those of us who find it a real turn-on to watch and/or participate with partners while they make love with others, Poly-O is the next best thing to heaven!

Another challenge of Poly-O Families is dealing with societal pressure. Plural Poly Pairs can "pass" as mono, making it easy to avoid problems with disapproving friends, parents, or employers. Poly-O members have to deal with what the local school will say when they enroll children and introduce their kids' two moms and three dads. To avoid this problem, some Poly-O Families choose to home school. Others designate specific legal parents for each child, usually one or both of the child's blood parents, and these parents are the only ones who interact with the school.

There is also the challenge of preparing children to get along with kids whose families are different from their own and whose parents may disapprove of polyamory. Children need to feel positively about their family, and hiding or keeping secrets from others implies a sense of shame. However, it is important for children to realize that out there in the big world, there are lots of different forms of families—single parents, kids being raised by an aunt or grandmother, same-sex parents, blended families, multi-partner families, and even occasionally heterosexual pair families—and that they are all totally acceptable.

Some Poly-O Families address the issue of privacy by teaching their children that there are things we openly share, and other things that are totally positive but simply nobody else's business. Sexuality generally fits into the latter category. "Mommy's other lovers" is a good example of something that is wonderful but private, so you don't discuss it at school or with other kids. Depending on the political and social climate of the community, families have to decide which aspects of their private life to encourage kids to keep private, thus avoiding discrimination and even possible legal threats to the family.

Legal and employment threats face all poly folks, especially those living in openly non-monogamous settings. We poly people have to remember that, thus far, there are no laws protecting our lifestyle from discrimination, including threats by well-meaning relatives or family services professionals who feel that a poly family is an immoral setting in which to raise children. Some poly families have faced legal action by relatives or ex-spouses intent on trying to take away their children. Employers may not take kindly to poly family pictures on desks, either. Until poly activists have succeeded in educating our society as a whole and obtaining legal protection for poly families, it's probably best to avoid confrontation, being totally open about the make-up of your poly family only with those you trust.

It is also important to take the legal steps necessary to protect shared property. Most Poly-O Families form a limited corporation, which holds the communal property. It is important to discuss all aspects of this arrangement among all family members first, then to find a lawyer who can be trusted and is familiar with non-traditional family forms. This can be a challenge, but poly organizations like Loving More can help with legal models and possible professional references. The family needs to discuss financial issues like what will happen if a family member decides to leave. Death is another inevitability. Without adequate legal contracts, if a poly family member dies and that person's share in the common property is inherited by non-poly-friendly children or relatives, it can cause major problems. Situations like this can and must be avoided by planning ahead and working with a good lawyer to create adequate documentation of the family's financial and legal issues.

Most effective ways of introducing new members into Poly-O Families

Inviting new members into a Poly-O Family is a group decision, based on consensus and a sense of whether the new person will fit into the family dynamics and benefit the entire family. This is quite different from the generally accepted model of courtship, which starts with physical attraction between two people, and culminates in a sexual and social partnership between the two of them, with little or no input from anyone else. Sure, physical attraction may be the first thing that makes one or more members of a Poly-O Family notice a new person, but someone does not generally become a new member based merely on their chemistry with one or more of the family members. Personality, skills, openness to the values of the group, and willingness to fit into the family dynamics are at least as important as hormonal attraction, if not more so.

Poly-O Families wanting to expand may look for new members at poly gatherings, on-line personals, or social events of people sharing the basic interests and values of the group. For example, a rural Poly-O Family that does organic farming and values green living might meet a potential new member at a workshop on green construction, holistic health, off-the-grid living, new farming techniques, or a environmental political action gathering.

Group courtship generally starts with doing things together and inviting the potential new member(s) to some family meals. As individual members of the family get to know the new person, the family observes the interactions and discusses how they feel about expanding the family circle. As in all poly relationships, sex is not the primary focus in choosing a new partner, although it certainly does make the entire process juicier!

Agreement issues for Poly-O Circles

A group contracts in Poly-O Families may be longer than those of other types of poly relationships, since individuals are involved with each other in a wide variety of ways. There may be more discussion about family finances and the rotation of taking out the garbage and doing the dishes than there is on the rotation of who sleeps with whom!

A primary issue is polyfidelity—will each person be sexual only with other members of the family, or is the family open to members having outside lovers? If the family is polyfidelitous, after the initial STI testing and wait period, there is less need for safer sex negotiations. Generally, the love and diversity within a Poly-O Family is enough to satisfy the sexual and emotional needs of all the members, and take all their available energy. Realistically, if a member of a Poly-O Family consistently desires the independence and freedom of individual outside relationships, it is likely that the group-oriented Poly-O is just not the right relationship form for them. These individuals may eventually migrate out of the family and into a more Poly-P lifestyle. Nevertheless, some Poly-O circles choose to be open, and if so, they must negotiate safer sex guidelines for activities outside the fluid-bonded family. Any open Poly-O Family will also have to negotiate all the communication issues discussed under Poly-P agreements—what information to share about outsiders and when, what input and/or veto power family members will have about outside lovers, etc.

As mentioned above, either in the family agreement or in separate legal negotiations, the group must negotiate financial assets and responsibilities, how they will deal with bringing new members into the family, both socially and financially, and what they will do if members leave and/or die. If children are part of the family, the contract will probably include issues regarding who the legal parents of the children are, and who will have guardianship should members leave the poly family.

Many groups agree on some communication guidelines, possibly some conflict resolution commitments and techniques, and spell out the group values upon which their family is based, be they spiritual, intellectual, social or environmental. Often agreements also include a clarification of space issues, specifying private areas and communal space and how these areas will be respected and maintained.

Some Poly-O agreements also address division of duties as well as time issues, such as how often they will set aside time for group discussions and shared meals. If there are children involved, issues about child rearing may also become a part of the group agreement. Some families use their contract to set aside specific times for group rituals and celebrations. All work and no play (or all processing and not enough cuddle time) can make a Poly-O Family way too cumbersome to last. But the opposite extreme, just hanging loose and going with the flow, is a sure recipe for group conflict. The key is making agreements fun and practical, and only adding new clauses when they are needed for the greatest common good.

Poly etiquette for members of Poly-O Circle Relationships

All of us have had experience living in an intimate multi-person family—we were born into one! So we already know that the first rules of family etiquette are mutual respect and individual responsibility.

Humor is another necessary point of etiquette that families often tend to forget. One group house I lived in had a member who tended to be pretty slack in his role in the kitchen. He often cooked his lunch then just left the remains in pans or plates on the table. After numerous family discussions about the issue, to no avail, the group stumbled onto what we still laughingly remember as the dead chicken cure. A family member came into the kitchen and once again found a pan of cold, greasy leftover fried chicken from Bob's lunch. He knew Bob was working late that night and would come home exhausted and flop into bed. The family member took the chicken, wrapped it in a paper towel, and put it under the covers in Bob's bed. Sure enough, at about midnight, the entire house was awakened by Bob's cry: "Damn, there's a dead chicken in my bed!" Everyone howled—and Bob quit leaving his dead food on the stove.

On a more serious note, etiquette requires following the group decisions regarding what and how much is shared outside the family. If some family members have jobs that might be in jeopardy if their employer disapproved of their being in a group relationship, then it is not polite to have group displays of affection in public places. For that matter, in any type of relationship, monogamous or polyamorous, a certain level of polite public discretion is generally appropriate.

In open Poly-O Families, it is polite to inform the rest of the family in advance if one is bringing a friend or a date home. Remember, although there is lots of love to go around, there is limited time and space. It is not polite to monopolize communal space entertaining or doing the courtship routine with a new date when other members of the family want to sit around the living room and chat about their day. Open Poly-O Families generally negotiate what space is open space, often choosing to do courtship outside the shared home or in the individual's private space.

It is a good idea to discuss how family members will refer to or introduce other family members to outsiders. Poly-O Families with children generally decide on names for the children to call the various adults: perhaps one is "mom," another "mama," and a third one "mother." Others use first names for all the family members rather than any parental nicknames. In most families, children are taught to obey all the adults in the group, but family etiquette tends to give the birth parent(s) greater authority in providing discipline and guidance. Just how this happens takes a fair amount of sensitivity and respect, and those are key factors in all etiquette.

Morphing to Poly-O from other forms of poly and to other models from it

Some people see the Poly-O Family as the most unique form of poly. They tend to think of the Poly-O Circle as the ultimate expression of polyamory, the relationship form toward which all the others aspire. I do not share this view. To me, each model has its own benefits and challenges, and none is intrinsically better or "more poly" than the others.

Whether or not Poly-O is the most unique form of poly, it is certainly the most complex and inclusive model. Therefore, given the fact that entropy is a basic law of both science and society, it is not likely that any of the smaller or simpler models will simply morph into a Poly-O naturally, without the input of energy and intention on the part of all the members of an existing relationship.

In general, the relationship form most likely to morph into a Poly-O Family is the Poly-Y Sensuous Network, especially if all the members of the network live in the same area and have a desire to spend an increasing amount of time with the other branches of the extended family.

On a smaller scale, a Poly-L Triad could add members, or cuddle up to another triangle, hypotenuse to hypotenuse, and form a Poly-O Circle. Of course, adding one member to a Triad morphs it into a Quad, and the Quad (a four-member poly family) is just a small Poly-O. But our goal is to identify patterns and themes within polyamory, not to analyze families and name their types. So whether a Quad is an extended Poly-L or a small Poly-O is a moot point. The only important thing is to understand that no matter how many members it has, the Poly-O Family is a totally inclusive form of polyamory.

The Poly-S Sensuous Chain is another poly form that could rather easily morph into a Poly-O if all its members developed a desire to interact with all the other members of the chain rather than merely with their adjacent partners.

In my experience, the poly form least likely to morph into a Poly-O is the Poly-P, due to the fact that the two forms are based on somewhat opposite values, individual independence vs. inclusive consensus. The type of person who prefers the autonomy inherent in the Porcupine Poly Pairs model might find the Poly-O too group-oriented and confining. Similarly, the inclusion-oriented person longing for a Poly-O tends to feel excluded from their partner's other relationships within Poly-P formats.

Needless to say, Poly-O Families sometimes break up, and when they do, they may sprout several of the other poly forms: a Poly-L Triad here, a Poly-S Sensuous Chain there, a Poly-P Plural Poly Pair or two there. Often, this occurs because members are tired of the hard work consensus requires and ready to form more independent couplings.

And then again, the entire entourage just might continue to stay in touch, morphing into a more loosely structured Poly-Y Network. Whatever the outcome, the dynamics of the Poly-O Circle are among the most interesting and complex of any in the poly community.

Chapter 5

L: The Loving Poly Triad

and the Non-Triadic V

L: The Loving Poly Triad
And the Non-Triadic V

The ménage à trois is another common form of poly family. In the poly community, the ménage à trois is often called a "V", but since there's no "V" in the word "polys," I simply rotated the "V" slightly to turn it into an "L". Three-way relationships are perhaps the most common small-family form of polyamory.

There are two different forms of this three-way relationship: the Poly-L Triad and the Non-Triadic Poly-L or "V". Although they are similar in that they both have three members, the dynamics of the two are quite different. In a "V", the Non-Triadic Poly-L relationship form, one person has two different lovers, but those lovers have no intimate relationship with each other, are not sexual with each other and may or may not have any emotional or social ties. It is possible, although not likely, that they do not even know each other. If they do, they may or may not like each other, although life is a lot easier if they are at least casual friends. Thus, the "L" or "V" is a derivation of the Poly-P, but with just two quills. Most of the information in Chapter 3 is therefore also applicable to the Non-Triadic Poly-L.

The Poly-L Triad, with a totally different feeling tone, is an extension of the "L" or "V" to form a triangle relationship in which all three people have strong ties emotionally, socially, sensuously, and often sexually as well. The Triad is a microcosm of the Poly-O Family. So just as Chapter 3 concepts fit the Non-Triadic Poly-L, much of the information in Chapter 4 is also applicable to Poly-L Triads. Triads tend to live together as an egalitarian family, sharing the job of child-rearing if children are part of the family. In many respects they are just like a traditional monogamous family, but with one more person.

The Poly-L Triad is a fairly common family form among both straights and bisexuals, as well as among gays and lesbians. Many polys embrace bisexuality, and the mixed-gender Poly-L Triad is an ideal family form for bisexual polys. But bisexuality is not a prerequisite for a mixed gender Triad. I'm not a great fan of family diagrams in which the connections are defined solely by who is sexual with whom, because in polyamory, emotional links are at least as important as sexual ones, possibly more so. My last Poly-L was a female-male-female Triad in which we two women were not sexual with each other, although we were bi-sensuous and enjoyed all playing together. We described our relationship as two overlapping "V"s in which the man was the vertex of the sexual "V", in that both of us women were sexual with him, while my female partner was the vertex of the emotional "V", in that both the male and I had stronger emotional connections to her than to each other. The Triad has gone separate ways, but the emotional link between us two women is still extremely strong, despite the many miles between us.

The Poly-L Triad has a long history. Just as Poly-P looks to *Open Marriage* for historical precedent, and Poly-O finds inspiration in *Stranger in a Strange Land,* a current book by Barbara and Michael Foster and Letha Hadady, *Three in Love, Ménages à Trois from Ancient to Modern Times,* is an interesting exploration of famous and not-so-famous people throughout history who have publicly or privately lived in Triad relationships. And although I have yet to hear a sermon on the topic, it is interesting to note that the three major western religions, Islam, Judaism and its offspring, Christianity, have their source in the Poly-L Triad of Abraham, Sarah and Hagar, as mentioned in Chapter 1. So the Poly-L Triad is a time-honored relationship form that remains common in the poly community.

Now let's take a look at the other threesome, the Non-Triadic Poly-L or "V". Although some Non-Triadic Poly-L relationships last for some time, and one or the other leg of the relationship may last for quite a while, this form as a threesome tends to be the most fluid and least stable form of poly, in my observation. There are several reasons. The person in the center has the job of meeting the emotional and sexual needs of two different people who may or may not be thrilled about sharing their partner with another lover, one they may not even know, and had no input in selecting. Therefore, many warn that the Non-Triadic Poly-L can be the form of poly that is the most prone to jealousy, competitiveness and drama.

The Non-Triadic Poly-L is a common starting relationship for monogamous couples taking their first steps into polyamory. It sometimes evolves from an old-fashioned "affair" which a supposedly-monogamous partner finally decides to quit hiding. The couple may have heard about polyamory, and the "cheating" partner may hope that, by embracing poly, they can keep both relationships going. This sometimes works, and sometimes does not. Either way, this is not the ideal way to transition into polyamory. We've quoted the old adage, "Don't study navigation in the middle of a storm." One committed lover is already dealing with the pain of finding out that their partner has been cheating. To then attempt to convince that person that polyamory will solve everything is not an ideal way to mutually choose to open up a marriage.

There is another way Non-Triadic relationships may end up being created. Unwary couples can make a wrong turn on their way to forming an inclusive Poly-L Triad, and end up in a non-inclusive, Non-Triadic "V" by mistake. Two primary partners may have decided to open up their relationship, with the goal of forming an inclusive Triad, perhaps even dreaming of eventually expanding to create an inclusive Poly-O Family. They make a commitment to search together for a new person they both like; someone whose energy resonates with both of theirs; someone who meets needs of both partners while they meet desires of the new partner; someone who wants to gradually meld into their family and become an intimate part of both of their lives. They commit to collaboration and egalitarian decision-making in choosing their new partner(s). Then one primary partner "jumps the gun" and does the old "I see her, I want her, I take her, I commit to her." After a few months, he brings her home to his primary, assuming the existing partner will immediately adore hot new love object and Poof, they'll be a big, happy, inclusive Poly-L Triad.

Once in a while this actually works, but more often the response from the existing primary partner is something akin to "So what am I, chopped liver? Which head were you thinking with, and how did you manage to forget our commitment to egalitarian decisions about who we bring into our lives? What made you forget that we committed to working together openly in building family, and to collaborating in choosing people we both genuinely enjoy, who enhance both of our lives while we enhance theirs? We agreed that we'd work together in the initial process of getting to know a potential new partner and finding out whether or not there is an interest in joining both of us to form the Loving Poly-L Triad we long to create together. But you leapt over the fence on your own, buddy! You picked her, she's yours, and you and she can pack up and move on down the pike, or at least carry on your relationship elsewhere."

I'm making this a bit more dramatic than it often ends up being, just to remind you that waiting a few more hours or days can be a good idea, in order to discuss the potential love with your primary partner. The two of you can then invite hot new love-potential home for dinner and gradually make a joint decision about inviting the person into your lives. This collaborative process results in a much greater likelihood of creating an inclusive Poly-L Triad than playing Lone Ranger and still expecting the results that come from collaboration.

Both short-term and longer-term Non-Triadic Poly-L relationships also exist among single polys who are dating around, searching for long-term relationships, and experimenting to find out what type of family they want to form once they find the special someone(s) they genuinely care for. The dynamics of polyamory among single people is discussed more fully in Chapter 8.

Despite the challenges that sometimes accompany a Non-Triadic Poly-L relationship, it can be an ideal form for some people. The Poly-L is a great relationship form if the two people who are the outside links of the "L" are rather independent souls who want love and romance in their lives but without the amount of time, commitment and communication necessary for a Poly-L Triad or Poly-O Family. It can be a great love situation for people who have exciting careers which require a great deal of their time and passion; for people who either have a relatively low sex drive or are happy to satisfy some of it with juicy solo sex; or for those who enjoy having a fair amount of time to be alone. Instead of meeting all the sexual and intimacy needs of a partner, let alone the needs of two or more partners, the person on the outside of a Poly-L has to meet only half of the intimacy needs of their partner, and has lots of personal freedom.

For people in the center of the "L", it may sound like a lot of fun to have two lovers all to themselves. But it can also be a lot of work to meet the emotional, sexual, and social needs of two different people, besides having a job and dealing with all the other responsibilities of life. However, this is a good position for a person who needs to be needed. It can also be a good fit for someone who prefers to split their time, energy, and commitment, but without spreading it around as much as a Poly Porcupine. The Non-Triadic Poly-L can also simply be a person's first step toward a Plural Pair Porcupine lifestyle. If life at the middle of a Non-Triad Poly-L feels good, moving on to being a full-fledged Porcupine may be the next step in finding the lifestyle that fits.

It is important for the person at the center of the "L" to remember the suggestions described in the Poly-P section about "tending your garden," especially when starting that new relationship. The other primary partner in Poly-P relationships is likely to also have other lovers, so is not as likely as the existing partner in a new Poly-L to be sitting home alone while their mate is out with a shiny new love object. Remember how it feels to be left out of the action, and be sure your partner sitting at home gets a little more than their share of the action once you get back from your date.

Just as one person in an "L" has to deal with the challenges of seeing their partner all excited about a new relationship and in the euphoria of NRE (new relationship energy), it can be an equally difficult challenge to comfort that same partner when the other relationship ends. There is a lot of freedom built into the Non-Triadic Poly-L, and while celebrating the freedom, be sure to think ahead about how to honor, nourish, celebrate with, and comfort your partners as relationships come and go, because this relationship form tends to have its share of coming and going,

Since most of the characteristics, agreement issues, benefits and challenges of the non-Triad Poly-L are essentially the same as those of the Poly-P Porcupine, they will not be repeated in this section. If you're interested, look back at the Poly-P descriptions in Chapter 3, and apply them to just two quills. For the rest of this chapter, we will instead focus on the dynamics of the Poly-L Triad.

Benefits of the Poly-L Triad

Since the communication and negotiation challenges in poly relationships increase exponentially with the number of partners, the small size of the Poly-L Triad is a definite advantage. Many people find that three is a magic number, providing diversity as well as intimacy.

Poly-L Triads are ideal for bisexuals, at least within FMF and MFM Triads. For a bisexual, it provides an ongoing relationship with both genders, rather than sequential relationships with same and different-gender partners. And many homosexual families find the Triad a wonderful way to have some diversity that is not available in a monogamous partnership without the safe sex challenges of casual partners or Poly-P relationships.

On the purely logistic side, it can be tough for a Poly-O Family to find a house that will work for them. But three loves can fit into most any house, especially if the master bedroom is big enough for a king-size bed! No complicated patterns for sexual rotation are necessary in a Triad. If the relationship is a sexual "L", the partner at the vertex can simply alternate beds and/or partners. And if they're a sexual triangle, the only rotation is who gets to be in the middle. (There is a popular poly tee shirt that shows three stick figures and has the message, "Tonight I get the middle!") The Triad offers most of the size convenience of the pair relationship, but with more diversity.

Poly-L Triads have a good track record for longevity. It is important to realize, however, that longevity alone is not a true measure of the value of a relationship. I've known some powerful relationships of all types that had wonderful quality and intensity, although they did not last for a huge number of years. But especially when a family is raising children, staying together over time helps provide security and continuity for children. Many Triad relationships I've known were formed with the specific goal of better meeting the challenges of child-rearing.

Time to be alone was mentioned as one of the benefits of the Poly-O model. The same can be said of the Poly-L Triad. I love traveling in a Triad format. I really value some time alone, and find that for me, Triads flow beautifully: A and B can do something together, giving C time alone, then B and C can go out leaving the privacy of the hotel room to A, then B gets privacy while A and C go out. Then we can all three be together. I love it!

Poly-L Triads seem to meet a lot of the pair-bonding needs that draw people to the coziness of monogamy, while at the same time providing room for a bit more diversity of personalities and interactions. The third person can be a great help when differences of opinion happen, which is inevitable in all relationships. When a pair, Parker and Payton, are in disagreement, it can lead to a built-in stalemate: "I guess I just see it this way, and you see it that way, and we're at loggerheads." A therapist is often called in to provide the cooler third voice. Triads have a built-in third voice, Pat, who loves both Parker and Payton and can observe, intercede, and mediate.

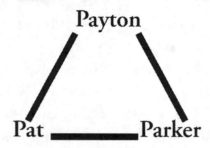

a Poly-L Loving Triad

A related dynamic is the need for feedback to facilitate personal growth. If there are just two in the relationship and Pat says to Parker, "I've been noticing that you shoot yourself in the foot by…" Pat may simply not see it that way, and once again, they are at loggerheads. But if Parker *and* Payton, both loving partners who know Pat well, hold up the same loving mirror, their feedback is more likely to be taken seriously and acted upon, nurturing Pat's personal growth as well as family cohesiveness.

Challenges within Poly-L Triads

In mixed gender Poly-L Triads, the single-gender partner does not have a sister-wife or brother-husband, which can make it a bit lonely. The single-gender partner can sometimes feel outnumbered, out-voted, or even ganged up on by the other two partners.

In polyfidelitous mixed-gender Poly-L families that are not sexual Triads, meeting everyone's needs can be a challenge. For example, in a FMF Triad, the solitary male may feel pressure to treat both of his female partners exactly the same, spending the same amount of sensuous and emotional time with each in order to meet all the sexual and social needs of both of his sensuous ladies. At times, he may wish he could call in reinforcements! Meeting the needs of two high-energy partners may sound like fun, but it can be a lot of work.

Gay and lesbian Triads sometimes face discrimination from gay friends and isolation from the rest of the GLBT community. I have three friends who are a poly gay Triad and have lived together for well over ten years. They tell me they get way more harassment from their gay friends for living together in a threesome than they get from the straight world for being gay.

As in the Poly-O Family, deciding whether the relationship is to be polyfidelitous or open is another challenge. It is especially difficult if some members would really like to keep it open, while others want to cozy down in an exclusive threesome. Like in all forms of polyamory, communication, honesty, and willingness to renegotiate the family agreements are essential.

If the Triad is open, then all the issues of space and time for dating outside people discussed in the Poly-O chapter need to be negotiated. Bringing others into the relationship threatens the format of a Triad, but that is not necessarily a bad thing. After all, each model can morph into another model, and variety is the spice of life, not only in lovers but in modes of loving as well. Discussing dreams and goals can help a threesome decide they want to reach out and morph into a larger Poly-O. On the other hand, they may want to have more freedom by morphing into a Poly-P Porcupine. Or perhaps they will enlarge their family by becoming a part of a Poly-Y tribe or a Poly-S Sensuous Snake, the two remaining poly forms that we will be discussing shortly.

Most effective ways of introducing new members

Once two singles who dream of being part of a Triad have found each other, the first miracle has happened, so the next is far more likely. Most couples discuss the types of qualities they're looking for in a third member. What needs is this person going to meet for each existing partner? What skills and interests will they add to the family? They also need to discuss each of their preferences for the gender of a third member. Whether or not one or both of the partners are bisexual will influence which gender they prefer to look for at poly gatherings and online personals. Most couples looking for a third do it together by meeting new people online or in person, inviting them to dinner, doing things together, and seeing how the dynamics flow among the three of them, in a manner very similar to that of a Poly-O Family. But once they have found someone, reaching consensus is easier because there aren't as many people involved.

Each partner going off to search on their own, like in a Poly-P model, is not nearly as likely to lead to a harmonious, egalitarian Triad. Beware of the all-too-common fantasy route, "I've found one sexy partner, so I'll just go out and find another I like, and when I've established a good, hot relationship with the second person, I'll just bring him/her home and introduce my new love, and I'm sure my two loves will instantly mesh and I'll be in heaven." Once in a while, in a fairy tale, that actually might happen, but it is more likely to be the beginning of your fantasy Triad morphing into the Plural Pair Porcupine model, which isn't all bad, but isn't where you thought you were going. It will most likely just land you in a classical "V", a Poly-L with two lovers who are not friends. And your primary partner may not be very happy that their dream of a loving Triad got co-opted by your impatience to find a second lover for yourself. Once again, communication, egalitarian decision-making, and clarity about your collaborative goals can avoid a lot of conflict and drama on the road to forming the poly family of your dreams.

However you choose to proceed, here is a foundational concept to remember: Since all forms of polyamory are ideally based on egalitarian decision making, the choice of a third partner is not likely to go smoothly if one person thinks the choice is primarily, or even initially, all his or hers to make. Most couples with success stories of bringing a loving third into their lives have done it together, with both of the initial partners having an equal say from the very beginning steps of the courtship.

Once a Triad is formed, bringing new members into the relationship is a moot point if the Triad is polyfidelitous and has no desire to morph into a larger family group. However, many Triads are not polyfidelitous and are open to morphing into a Quad or other relationship form. If this is the case, bringing new members in will again be best accomplished by working together collaboratively, inviting potential people to become family friends first, and then taking appropriate steps from there.

Agreement issues in Poly-L Families

By now, it may seem that there's nothing more to say about contracts. Like in the Poly-P model, both non-polyfidelitous open Triads and Non-Triadic Poly-L partners need to negotiate safer sex practices and communication issues regarding when and how much to share about outside loves. An open Triad can function as a three-way Plump Porcupine, each member having outside relationships, sometimes functioning as secondary or tertiary relationships, or just plain giggle-sex buddies. The more outside relationships members have, the more the Poly-L or Triad starts to function like our next form, the Poly-Y sensuous network or tribe.

A Triad faces the same financial and legal challenges as the Poly-O, but in a smaller format. It tends to be a bit easier for a Triad to draw up the legal papers to control joint property and address inheritance, finances, and all the things that are provided to married partners just by getting a marriage license. For models of financial partnerships, and suggestions of open-minded lawyers in your area, Triads often contact their local PFLAG (Parents and Friends of Lesbians And Gays), as the GLBT community has put a lot of work into helping each other establish safe legal protections for their partners.

Family finances, the sharing of chores, and issues relating to child rearing if the family includes children, also need to be addressed in the family agreement.

Poly etiquette within the two Poly-L models

We addressed the issue of primary and secondary relationships in the first chapter. Some poly folks abhor these terms, claiming that they love all their partners equally. Others find that being clear about time and commitment priorities within their family is vital to each person's knowing how to function securely. Many find that the terms "primary" and "secondary" provide this clarity. For many poly folks, knowing and being comfortable with one's position as a primary or a secondary is helpful in establishing family etiquette. In this arena, we can learn a lot from the world of BDSM (Bondage/Discipline, Dominance/Submission, Sado/Masochim, often also referred to as "kink"). Not only are roles both chosen and well-defined in the kink world, but contracts are common, virtually required, and they are usually carefully negotiated and religiously followed. There is safety in knowing the role one plays in a group, and that one has freely chosen that role.

In some Triads, especially mixed gender Poly-L's, one of the same-gender partners is primary and the other is secondary. This is common when one person is new to the relationship, when a single person joins a married or committed couple, when the third person lives some distance away and they are only together periodically, or possibly when the three are living together on a trial basis. It has always been my experience when entering a relationship with an established couple, that everything flows much more harmoniously if I consider my same-gender partner in the primary couple the conductor of the ensemble. A part of the etiquette of the secondary is to keep antennae out for the comfort level of the primaries, especially the same-gender primary. Any sense of competitiveness, discomfort or jealousy is a signal to slow down and take time to discuss how things are going for each one of you.

There are some points of etiquette during the initial courtship phases that bring powerful long-term benefits. Ideally, a couple will go through the phases of courting and getting to know a potential third member together. However, as was discussed in the Poly-P section, let us assume that Pat, one member of the couple we met above, chooses to act in a more Porcupine-like style, initiating one-on-one courtship with Payton. Then it is not only polite but extremely wise for Payton to respond to Pat's assurance that Parker is totally supportive of Pat starting this relationship with a statement such as, "I'm sure you're right, so let's get together with Parker so she can tell me herself that she's interested in my getting to know you better." If Pat objects, or runs away tail between legs, Payton has avoided potential drama. And if Pat is hoping for an eventual Triad, Payton's suggestion that Parker be included from the very beginning prevents Parker from feeling isolated, ignored, and left out of the courtship ritual.

If the potential secondary, Payton, does not make the suggestion of contacting Parker, then the primary partner, Pat, should certainly suggest it. Otherwise, the group is headed toward the bumpy Non-Triadic waters of the exclusive pair of relationships in the Non-Triadic Poly-L. Ideally, before things go much further between Pat and Payton, Parker and Payton will also make time to be together. The more all three are on the same page, getting acquainted at the same rate, the more likely the relationship is to work.

Some people find it difficult to remain a secondary forever. Most long-term Triads function on the basis of everyone eventually becoming co-primaries. However, while one is a secondary, poly etiquette requires respect for the primary and deferring to the primary, especially in issues of time and priority of needs. On the other hand, the sensitive primary will not play "Queen Bee" excessively. The primary needs to be respectful and open with the secondary; to see that the secondary's needs are considered, even though they do not take priority; to welcome the secondary; to make time for the secondary relationship to grow; and to nourish and support it, doing nothing to undermine it. Similarly, it is essential for secondaries to look honestly within themselves to be sure they are not harboring secret hopes of displacing the primary partner or doing anything to undermine the primary relationship. The role of the secondary is to *enhance* the primary relationship, to add to it and make it juicier, and to bring joy to all three partners. Anything any member does which does not enhance the primary relationship is bound to be a sure step to disaster.

So what does the secondary get out of this? Some websites are full of postings from secondary lovers whining about how tough it is to play second fiddle. Hey, if you don't want the job, don't apply for it! I personally love the position of secondary. Although a secondary in a Poly-P or Poly-L relationship gets considerably less time than the primary, it is often real fun quality time, not time spent dealing with all the routine issues that people living together need to deal with, like family finances and who takes out the garbage. Furthermore, the secondary has nearly as much personal freedom as a single person, while still having the warmth of an ongoing relationship. In a more inclusive Poly-L or a Triad, the friendship with the other primary is an added benefit for the secondary. As I see it, the secondary gets a lot of juiciness and love without having to deal with the domestic drudgery of picking up the dirty socks!

The issue of triangulation, which was defined and discussed in Chapter 3, is especially important in three-way relationships. It is never polite for two partners to talk about the third behind that person's back. Not only does this break the principles of etiquette, but it can also totally undermine the trust and personal growth of the relationship. Feedback about any member of a family needs to be shared with that member, not with someone else, no matter what form of polyamory or friendship exists. In my last Poly-L Triad, during our formation period we lived a long way from each other, so a lot of our communication was via email. We avoided triangulation and facilitated inclusive communication by copying the other partner on all emails any of us sent to each other. This is an easy way to keep everyone in the loop, assuring that nobody is being talked about behind their back, and preventing anyone from feeling isolated or left out.

I know many Triads who live close to each other, perhaps even sharing the same house, but who still follow this pattern, especially when communicating about important or controversial issues. Sometimes putting things in writing, with copies to all family members, serves two purposes. It gives us time to look at what we're saying, be sure it is not a rant or something blurted out in anger, and to check for clarity and legitimacy before clicking "send". It also provides a record to refer to in the future. Clear communication is a cardinal foundation of good etiquette and harmonious family living, and putting important communication into writing helps achieve this vital goal.

Morphing to Poly-L models from other forms of poly and to others from them

The Poly-L Triad can be a very stable relationship, as firm a basic building block as the monogamous couple. In addition, the Triad is an especially satisfying relationship pattern for bisexuals. Many Triads have little or no desire to morph into anything else. However, just as monogamy doesn't always wear well in mono couples, polyfidelity sometimes has limited longevity in Poly-L relationships.

Of course, there is a difference between gay or bisexual Poly-L Triads in which every member has two lovers, and strictly heterosexual ones where one member has two lovers and the other two have only one. In a Non-Triadic Poly-L, in time, one or both of the partners at the ends of the formation may develop a desire for another lover. The same can happen in a heterosexual Poly-L Triad. When this happens, the Poly-L may morph into a Poly-Y intimate network or a Poly-S chain of loves.

On the other hand, in two-gender Poly-L's, the single gender partner may start to feel like odd-one-out and suggest the addition of another family member, changing the Poly-L into a MFMF Quad, which is actually a small Poly-O. Quads tend to also be stable, many lasting for years. They provide the benefit of being able to "pass" as two couples simply sharing a house, or being next-door neighbors. The Quad is also a comfortable form for people who prefer one-on-one pair sexuality to three-in-a-bed sex or alternate nights alone. Of course, Quads can continue to expand, eventually becoming a larger Poly-O Family, a Poly-Y intimate network or a Poly-S sensuous snake.

Some Poly-L Triads decide on a different route to diversity by adding secondary relationships, thus morphing the Poly-L Triad into a three-cornered Poly Porcupine. Since the outside partners may also have partners of their own, this may progress into a Poly-Y intimate network.

What types of relationships morph into Triads? Sometimes a larger network breaks down into smaller families, as mentioned in the Poly-O section. More often, initially monogamous couples decide to open their relationship, but don't want to deal with the separate relationships of the Poly-P model. Especially if one or the other partner is exploring bisexual desires, searching for one additional partner can be a good way of expanding without adding numerous partners, thus keeping the family small and intimate.

We in the poly world haven't had a vocabulary to describe the various types of patterns within the plethora of polyamorous relationship types. Often a Poly-L or Triad just happens, with the same magic that occurs at the start of all relationships. Hopefully, with an increased vocabulary for investigating our own fantasies for family and an increased ability to share these dreams with our partner(s), the random magic of relationship forming and morphing can become more intentional and even more successful.

Chapter 6

Y: Yikes – Lots of Poly-Ls and Poly-Ps

Branching into Sensuous Networks, Webs, or Tribes

Y: Yikes – Lots of Poly-Ls and Poly-Ps
Branching into Sensuous Networks, Webs, or Tribes

In some areas of the world of technology, "Y" is a symbol for network. Therefore, it is an ideal symbol for the often expansive network of sensuous relationships that result from a dynamic such as the following:

Let's say that Jessie has a primary relationship with Leslie, and a secondary relationship with Sage, forming a "V" relationship. Soon, Jessie adds another secondary relationship with Jordan, transforming the "V" into a "Y". Then Leslie starts relationships with Logan and Lonnie, creating another "Y". By this time, Sage has formed relationships with Sidney and Shannon, creating another "Y". It is only a matter of time until Jesse's lover, Jordan, falls in love with Jackie, and then with Jaime, who has two lovers, Justice and Jude. The Poly-Y is far easier to draw than to describe. Jessie's relationships are the core of a relationship pattern like the diagram on the title page of this chapter. As you can see, a Poly-Y is an expansive, intimate network of relationships.

The Poly-Y can become nearly as far-reaching as the internet, and as impossible to limit or control. It is the most flexible and amorphous of all poly forms. The network or tribe is always changing and expanding, new lovers being added and, at times, existing love links changed, exchanged, or dropped. It is rather like a tree that branches in seemingly random and ever-expanding ways, remaining vital and alive despite some leaves and branches falling off now and then.

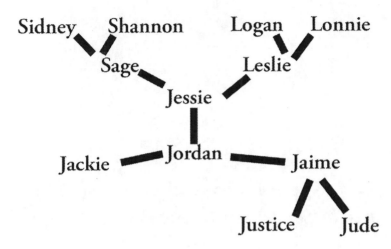

a Poly-Y Sensuous Network or Tribe

Needless to say, a Poly-Y tribe seldom lives in the same house. Some extend across vast distances, even different countries. Among smaller networks, everyone may know at least the names of all the other members, and they may attempt to all get together for special days, such as Thanksgiving. Some larger tribes that are spread across vast distances have set up list-serves to keep in touch with each other. Others just hang loose and continue expanding, with communication generally taking place only among members of individual branches.

Some tribes, like the Erosong Tribe based in Seattle but with branches extending to California and Hawaii, have a tribal identity, thanks to their poly activism and online presence. Other intimate webs are simply random networks of friends and lovers.

Benefits of the Poly-Y Network

Members of Poly-Y networks have all the benefits of their closest formations, the Poly-P and Poly-L or Triad, but with the added benefits that come with being part of a larger network of people. In addition to the freedom and intimacy of their own poly family, they can network with a constantly increasing number of like-minded people who are only a few degrees of separation away from themselves and their own lovers, if they choose to do so. Networks can be powerful communication assets, support systems in times of need, and social activism powerhouses. They can also be a source of new friends and lovers, as well as a trustworthy group of people with whom to share ideas and questions regarding the many joys and challenges of the poly lifestyle.

Connections between the various members of a Poly-Y network vary greatly. Some networks exist by mere chance, the Poly-Y having resulted from lovers adding other lovers to their lives without any implicit attempt to form an extended family or tribe. In these somewhat random networks, there may be little if any attempt to create a group identity or to establish communication among members. Other Poly-Y networks, like the Erosong tribe mentioned above, consider themselves a far-reaching family, many of the members having personal, social and/or sexual relationships with other members, and all knowing each other to some extent. I've been at workshops where Erosong members introduce their tribe by drawing a family tree diagram of the linkages, both sexual and emotional, between all the various members. They are active politically in the poly community, and a number of their members are leading poly educators and activists.

Flexibility is definitely an asset within Poly-Y networks or tribes. They provide those who long for extended family with some of the benefits of the Poly-O without the need to reach consensus over issues or to find a house big enough to fit everyone. Sometimes, in Poly-Y groups that maintain close connections and consider themselves a tribe or community, various family groups help each other in a myriad of ways, possibly including child care. Some gather to help a member group establish a new home or farm, while others share common financial endeavors or businesses. However, formal financial bonds are the exception rather than the norm in Poly-Y networks.

Regardless of how intimate or casual the network, social and emotional support of individual members is quite common. If a partner dies or is ill, often far-flung members of the tribe will come to the aid of the grieving or ill member and their core family. Often tribes help each other in times of financial crisis, as well as providing support in legal battles or political efforts to further the cause of poly freedom.

Challenges facing members of Poly-Y Networks

Confidentiality can be a challenge to members of a Poly-Y network, especially for someone who is not "out" as poly due to professional or personal concerns. The more people who know you are poly, the more likely your name is to pop up in casual conversation as being associated with the poly community. I actually know at least one person who has adopted a pseudonym which she uses exclusively in all her interactions in the poly community, just to be sure there is no chance of people in her professional world being able to google her real name and find any poly connections. There are currently no laws protecting poly individuals or families from discrimination in work, housing, or child custody issues. So even though you might like to be "out of the closet" as poly, and to make political statements about your poly status, it is wise to consider the implications if you have children or a job that might be at risk. Using a different name socially can be a solution, although that might cause a feeling of having a split identity. Another even more far-reaching solution is to use the power of networks, both formal and informal, to work together to educate society about the existence of healthy poly families, and to work to change discriminatory laws and practices.

Although most Poly-Y webs do not actually get together on any regular basis, one challenge that can face those who do long to all be together is the difficulty of finding space for gatherings of such a large group. In a society as mobile as ours, even if the tribe started out in a single location, it is likely that in time it will become far-flung, so travel expenses can make it difficult to all get together. That is why the internet has become the family gathering of choice for many Poly-Y sensuous networks.

The same challenges of triangulation that face Poly-L formations can expand exponentially if gossip gets a chance to infest a Poly-Y tribe. Chapters 3 and 4 defined and discussed this destructive form of non-inclusive communication. There are actually a few Poly-Y networks who follow the habit of copying all communications to all members, but this can cause massive inbox jams if the web becomes large. So good sense and positive communication skills are the best way to avoid the problem of triangulation.

Safer sex issues are just as essential among non-fluid-bonded members of Poly-Y networks as they are in any other type of relationship. The agreements of the inner family must be followed, no matter how much one sees other members of the tribe, because the network will tend to keep expanding, continuing to bring new risk factors into the mix. Very few Poly-Y tribes are polyfidelitous and fluid-bonded, so safer sex practices are still necessary among extended members of the same tribe.

Most effective ways of introducing new members into Poly-Y Webs

Except in small Poly-Y tribes which choose to function almost like a Poly-O, there are no particular protocols for introducing new members into Poly-Y networks. Each component Poly-P or Poly-L family will follow its own agreement and etiquette in bringing in new members into its intimate circle. Then, if the Poly-Y has a group listserv or website, once a new relationship has been established, the new person's lover or family will probably introduce the newcomer online.

A few Poly-Y networks seem to have a key member, perhaps the person who initially had the vision or dream of the tribe, or the longest-standing member of the group, who maintains a casual diagram of the family. If so, that person adds new members to the diagram, and deletes members if they leave the group. However, most Poly-Y networks are pretty loosely connected and casual, so new members are welcomed informally if at all, and leaving members are missed primarily by their own intimate family, without any major event to note the change in the family diagram.

Agreement issues in Poly-Y Tribes

Since most Poly-Y networks are very loosely structured, or not structured at all, the only agreement issues are those of the individual families that make up the larger network. Since respect for diversity is a key value within polyamory, it is not uncommon to find a variety of types of poly formats existing within the same Poly-Y. A network may contain some Poly-P Pairs, some Non-Triadic Poly-L "V" links, some Poly-L Triads, a Poly-S Sensuous Snake or two, and possibly even an open Poly-O, each with its own unique set of agreements or contracts.

Some Poly-Y networks establish confidentiality agreements regarding what is shared among tribe members but not with outsiders. There are even Poly-Y networks which have been together long enough that they have become polyfidelitous, and are thus fluid-bonded among the tribe members. If any part of the network is open, however, they must have firm safer sex contracts regarding sexual activity.

Poly etiquette in Poly-Y Networks

The cardinal rule of etiquette within Poly-Y networks is non-triangulation. One of the main functions of a Poly-Y network is to provide mutual support for all its members. Within an extended network, triangulation can quickly expand into harmful gossip, which can change a loving network into a toxic environment. Yes, tribes often take on problems and issues, but the focus is on solving group and interpersonal problems in a way that respects each person, focusing on the issues rather than the mistakes or flaws of an individual. If interpersonal problems are seen as challenges that we all face as we attempt to create new relationships for which we have few positive role models, they can be addressed as a communal challenge in which we are all working to support each other. With this approach, it is never the goal to point a finger at any individual or their behavior.

Being there for the other members of the tribe, both in times of need and in times of celebration, is an important aspect of tribe membership. Respecting the confidentiality of each member is another point of etiquette in Poly-Y networks, as is respect for the freedom and privacy of each member. It is sometimes easy to think that, just because we are part of the same network, we have special rights with respect to rather distant members in the tribe, while in fact that is not the case. For example, just because a person is a member of another family grouping within one's tribe does not mean that they are open to being sexual. Respecting the various and varying agreements of individual families or partnerships within the tribe, especially when they are different from our own, is an important part of the respect that makes the tribe a model of the wealth of diversity that polyamory can provide.

Morphing to Poly-Y Webs from other forms of poly and to others from it

Some poly folks start out with the desire to form a tribe or some type of rather large intentional community. Some start out hoping for a Poly-O, and discover that consensus decision-making is just too difficult, so morph into a more loosely knit Poly-Y type of extended family made up of a network of smaller family units. Others start small, and at some point discover that their social, sexual, and emotional network has expanded without their particularly intending it to do so. Poly-Y webs tend to be constantly morphing to and/or from other forms of polyamory. It can be beneficial, in my opinion, to make the development of an extended network of intimate connections conscious and intentional rather than just allowing it to happen with no awareness or purpose.

Non-intentional Poly-Y networks are most likely to evolve from Poly Porcupine relationships in which very little about secondary lovers is shared. Secondary partners may follow the pattern and also share very little about their other relationships. A network of lovers is created, whether or not any of them are aware of it. There may be no desire to nurture the network that exists among one's lovers. But, in my opinion, it is a shame for such a potentially powerful network, with all the social and political benefits it could have, to remain unknown and unused. Furthermore, this unknown web of relationships can lead to some surprising or embarrassing encounters, especially in relatively small communities. People in more inclusive Poly-P, Poly-L relationships and open Triads tend to know more about their partner's partners, so those relationship patterns are more likely to morph into intentional Poly-Y networks.

Although less common, a Poly-Y network can form rather spontaneously from an intimate group of friends who for years have gone places together and done things as a group. This is common among today's young people, who are much less likely to pair off and "go steady" with a single partner than was the norm in earlier generations. A group of youth who hang out together may eventually form internal partnerships of various types, but still feel a strong sense of group identity and enjoy doing things all together, thus evolving into a network that functions like a Poly-Y. This group focus is likely to make polyamory itself a more acceptable social form in the future than it is among the current adult society, which grew up in a more strongly pair-limited social setting.

Some Poly-Y networks form through the internet and conferences. Individual poly families may meet other families at a conference, stay in contact via the internet, and eventually form connections between members, leading to a Poly-Y network emerging. Some might claim that the entire poly community is a very loosely connected Poly-Y, in that many of us form social and emotional bonds across vast distances through poly chat rooms and other forms of global communication.

As we continue to expand through local poly discussion groups and poly education, we are becoming a powerful web of activism for social change in our society, challenging people to make conscious choices about their own relationship forms, and nurturing a greater acceptance of diversity.

Chapter 7

S: Sensuous Poly Snakes

L to N to W and Beyond, toward Daisy-Chain O

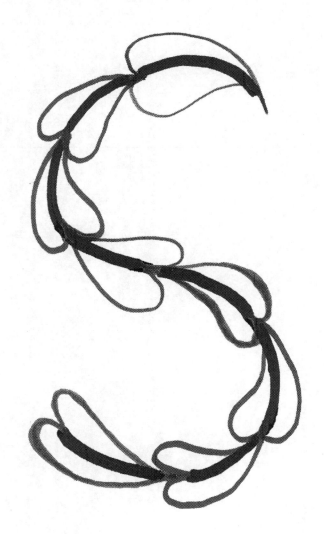

S: Sensuous Poly Snakes
L to N to W and Beyond, toward Daisy-Chain O

The Sensuous Poly Snake is not a terribly common form of poly relationship, but it is so interesting that it needs to at least be mentioned. A Poly-S Sensuous Snake or Poly Chain might be thought of as an extension of a Poly-L. Ready for some alphabet soup? Okay, let's start with a Non-Triadic Poly-L or "V". Let's say Casey is in the middle of the "V" and has two partners, Bobbie and Devin. Eventually, Bobbie forms a relationship with Ali. This four-person non-Quad type relationship is now usually referred to as "N" because the shape of that letter can be used as a diagram of the relationships between Ali and Bobbie, Bobbie and Casey, Casey and Devin. What if Devin now starts a relationship with Erin? This five-way relationship can be referred to as a "W." If it grows further, with Erin forming a relationship with Freddie, we run out of letters with an appropriate shape to diagram it, so it is simply called an "S" or poly chain. I use the Poly-S to represent a chain-type relationship of any size larger than the three people of a Poly-L or "V".

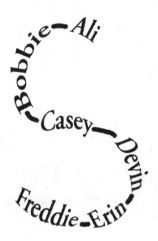

a Poly-S Sensuous Poly Snake

How does a Poly-S chain differ from a Poly-O? They are similar in that, unlike in a Poly-P, all the people involved know each other, are most likely friends, and may actually do things together as a group at times. However, in a Poly-O, all the members are emotionally and possibly also sexually involved with each other, while in a Poly-S chain each of the partnerships is basically a pair relationship with the two people on either side of them in the chain. In other words, Bobbie is a pair with Ali as well as with Casey, Casey is a pair with Bobbie as well as with Devin, and so forth, but there is no special intimacy between Bobbie and Erin, Ali and Devin, Ali and Erin, or Casey and Freddie.

Confusing? Well, let's look at a particular example: a group of professors who teach at the same university. Addison is married to Blake; Campbell is married to Dominique; Emerson is divorced and has joint custody of the kids, who are with him alternate nights. Emerson is intimate with Dominique and Campbell is intimate with Blake, so they have worked out a rotation. On Monday, Emerson has his kids and each of the married couples are at home with their legal spouses. But on Tuesday when Emerson's kids are with his ex-wife (who is not poly), Dominique sleeps at Emerson's house and Blake spends the night at Campbell's house. On Wednesday, things go back to the Monday status, and on Thursday, they go back to the Tuesday status. This has gone on for about a dozen years, with none of them being "out" as poly on their jobs. They are able to "pass" as two long-term married couples who are good friends with each other and another professor, who happens to be divorced.

The Poly-S is a good relationship for married couples who prefer primarily pair-based relationships, but do not want the number of different pairs that often exist with Poly-P couples. Since Poly-P and Poly-S are both pair-based, they are the two forms of poly which are most appropriate for people who, for personal or professional reasons, wish to live a lifestyle that looks to outsiders like a monogamous marriage. After all, most married couples have other married friends who come over for dinner regularly. I often wonder how many of the "normal" married couples out there are secretly practicing polyamory during those dinner parties and bridge nights!

Not everyone might relish the regular house-swapping that the couples in my example have chosen, but it works for them and a lot of other Poly-S extended families. The regularity of the rotation is a lot simpler than the constant calendar negotiation most Poly-P people deal with in order to schedule dates with their various outside partners. The Poly-S relationship can provide the social and professional safety of monogamy as well as the sexual and emotional variety of polyamory, all within a close-knit social circle of good friends.

Benefits of the Poly-S Model

The Poly-S provides both variety and security, while avoiding the potential drama and work involved in searching for unrelated outside loves. It provides a network of friends, without the level of togetherness and consensus decision-making of the Poly-O. It can be quite stable and fulfilling, thus providing a good chance for longevity. It is also an ideal format for families with children, as the children live in their own home, and to the outside world, their family appears to be a normal, monogamous family. Therefore, they do not face the questions and possible disapproval of friends and their parents who do not understand multi-partner families. They do not have to deal with a variety of other partners coming into and out of their lives, as the Poly-S provides an extended network of close adult friends who all do things together, with only one other person spending the night. So Poly-S tends to be less confusing to kids than the Poly-P or Poly-O might be.

As mentioned above, this model of poly is ideal for couples who want or need to be fairly circumspect regarding their polyamorous activities, as it's easy to pass as married couples who have a circle of other married couples as friends. Some Poly-S chains set up regular rotations, like the example discussed, which can vastly simplify scheduling of outside dates. Since, unlike Poly-P folks, everyone tends to be social friends, it also avoids the "who do I get to be with on holidays" challenge which often leaves secondaries alone on special days. It's common for good friends to spend holidays together, so nobody thinks much about it when everyone meets at one couple's house for Thanksgiving.

Another advantage of the Poly-S is that, while in a Poly-P and the Non-Triadic Poly-L, the primary is left at home alone when their partner goes out on dates, in the rotating Poly-S, the only people who are sometime left all alone are the ones whose position is at either end of the chain. Of course, in an ideal world, Ali would fall in love with Zeus (or whatever initial is at the end of the Poly-S chain) thus turning the Poly-S into a complete daisy chain. Alas, this does not always happen, so those at both ends of the chain have some time without a partner, which they may well enjoy using to focus on their kids, friends, pet projects, or just luxuriating in peace and solitude. Or, in time, they may find another partner for themselves, thus extending the chain. Thus, an end position on a Poly-S chain is a great position for a person who wants the benefits of a stable ongoing relationship and membership in a loving group, combined with the freedom to date other people.

Challenges of the Poly-S Model

The balance between spouse and lover provided by the Poly-S, although being one of the strengths of the model, can also be a challenge, in that the balance is endangered if a person in the middle of the chain decides to take on additional lovers. But flexibility tends to be a hallmark trait among polys of all types. So with good communication and sensitivity to the needs of existing members, added lovers do not have to constitute a problem, so long as the time spent seeing them does not interrupt the routines established by the primary partners in the Poly-S. After all, there are such things as afternoon delights, which can provide lots of time for outside loves without upsetting an evening rotation schedule. But in reality, for people with challenging jobs and other interests, a spouse and one other regular lover just could be sufficient.

Of course, not all Poly-S chains work out rotational schedules quite as regular as in the example. Without a set schedule, dividing time fairly can become as intricate a challenge as it is for Poly

Porcupines, especially if everyone is trying to fit nights with lovers into the same night their spouse is spending with their lover.

Although being at the end of the chain brings specific challenges, regular time alone is not all bad. A position at the end of the chain provides time to pursue ones own interests as well as greater freedom and support in looking for new loves, if that's what one wants to do.

Most effective ways of introducing new members

Just as Triads and Quads can develop among people who work together, go places together, or are neighbors or social acquaintances, Poly-S relationships can also evolve from simple friendships. As friendships develop into sexual partnerships, communication and mutual consent are vital, as is the case in all poly relationships.

Since many Poly-S chains have a fair degree of longevity, there are not as many issues regarding introducing new members, except when a member decides to take additional lovers. If a person at the end of the chain meets a new person, that person generally only needs to be introduced to that person's other partner or spouse, although if they become a regular lover, they will probably meet all the other members eventually.

Agreement issues in Poly-S Families

Once members have been tested and have satisfied the wait time, safer sex is usually not a consideration. However, any sex with people outside the fluid-bonded chain requires the same type of agreements as in all other forms of poly.

Communication about who and when to tell about a potential new love is a bit different from either the Poly-P or the Poly-O. In the Poly-P, other secondaries often know very little about new secondaries, with the exception of perhaps knowing that a new person has become part of the group. Even among Poly-Porcupines where the primary has veto power, it is uncommon for other secondaries to have veto power or even input into the selection of new lovers. The opposite of this is the Poly-O where everyone gets to meet a potential new lover and everyone has a say about whether or not to invite the new person to become part of the family.

The Poly-S is rather at a mid-point of these two extremes. Generally, potential new members are introduced only to the primary partner, in the case of people at the end of the chain, but soon meet the others. Some smaller chains operate more like a small Poly-O, however, and introduce any potential new love to everyone and ask for input. Their agreement ideally spells out the group's preferences on input and communication regarding potential new loves.

Poly etiquette in Poly-S Families

Triangulation is perhaps the first point of etiquette for members of a Poly-S Sensuous Chain. It is impossible for everyday conversation not to include mentions of other loves, since everybody knows everybody. But it is never appropriate to take problems with one lover to the other lover rather than addressing the issue directly with the person involved. It is common for partners to invite the other lover to join them in a discussion, as the added perspective can be of great value. The cardinal rule, however, is that relationship issues are discussed face to face, and never behind anyone's back.

Another issue of etiquette, especially in models where there are house-to-house rotations, is for the primary partner to welcome the lover and provide some space for them to leave a few personal things, like a robe and toothbrush, so the rotating lover does not feel as if they're forever on the road. On the other hand, the "visiting" love should be respectful of the belongings of the primary partner who lives there. It can drive one crazy to come back to one's kitchen and find that another person using it has put everything away in totally different drawers and cabinets. Simple respect and attention to space issues can avoid conflict and drama.

Morphing to a Poly-S from other poly forms and to other models from it

Sometimes a long-term Poly-S evolves into a Poly-O, with all the members becoming such close friends that they want to share intimacy, emotionally and/or physically, with all the other members of the chain. On the other hand, sometimes a Poly-S Chain breaks up, leaving an assortment of Pairs, Triads, or perhaps even a Quad or two. A third option is that some members of the chain may develop other loves, morphing the Poly-S into the core of a Poly-Y sensuous network.

It is less likely for a Poly-S to morph into a Poly-P format, as there is not a core pair and the relationships are already among close friends. So chances are that they will not turn into the disconnected pairs of porcupine quills in Poly Porcupine relationships.

Chapter 8

Choices

Dreams, Fantasies and Life Goals

Choices
Dreams, Fantasies and Life Goals

After looking at all these poly relationship choices, you may be feeling like a kid in a candy store! Most of us grew up with only two options for our relationship future. Ideally, we would get married, have kids, and have a life that looked fairly similar to that of our own family, or the families we saw all around us, in our school books and on television. Perhaps we didn't want a family quite like the one we grew up in, but were sure we'd pick the right person and create a better relationship than our parents did. The other option, way less favorable, was that of staying single, being an "old maid" (remember that term?) or a lonely old man. We may have reframed the options of the single life, choosing to be a glamorous career girl or a care-free bachelor. But whatever you called it, staying single meant living alone for our entire lives.

Back in 1982, futurist John Naisbitt's well-known book, *Megatrends,* presented ten major trends Naisbitt saw as defining the future of our culture. The final chapter, "Trend #10: Either/Or to Multiple Options" begins:

> Personal choices for Americans remained rather narrow and limited from the postwar period through much of the 1960's. Many of us lived the simple lives portrayed in such television stories as *Leave it to Beaver* and *Father Knows Best*: Father went to work, mother kept house and raised 2.4 children. There were few decisions to make; it was an either/or world:
> * Either we got married or we did not (and of course, we almost always did).
> * Either we worked nine to five (or other regular full-time hours) or we didn't work, period.
> * Ford or Chevy.
> * Chocolate or vanilla.

…one thing is clear: The traditional nuclear family (which has always depended on the wife subordinating too many of her individual interests to those of her husband and children) seems unlikely to return any time soon (pg. 231, 236).

Polyamory is, to me, one of many pieces of evidence that show Naisbitt's prediction coming true. Not only does polyamory provide an alternative to the either/or option of the single life or married monogamy, but it also includes a wide variety of relationship options within the polyamorous lifestyle itself.

And while we're on the subject of the single lifestyle, let's talk about the options available today for single people in each of the partnership forms we've discussed. We've used the word "family" quite a bit, and if you're single, you may be thinking that once again, the single person is left out in the cold. No way! I know a lot of polyamorous people who are single by choice, love being single, and find polyamory to be a wonderful lifestyle for the single person.

Single and Polyamorous

So how does each of the models fit the single person? Perhaps most obvious is the role of a single person as a secondary in one, or several, Poly-P constellations. As I mentioned before, I love being a secondary because it gives me nearly all the freedom of a totally unattached single life, plus the warmth and connection of a possibly long-term relationship. I have a friend who, after a number of years of marriage, decided she had no desire for a primary relationship, preferring the freedom of the single life. She has several lovers, spread across two coasts and several countries. In each of her relationships, she is a secondary in a very open, inclusive Poly-P type formation with married poly couples. Although she sees each of her lovers only periodically, she is friends with each of their wives, and stays in close phone and email contact with both partners in each of her poly relationships. She has her own career, comes home to her own little house most nights, makes her own decisions and her own travel plans—and has only her own dirty socks to pick up!

The Poly-O may include individuals who are not legally or emotionally married, but they are definitely part of an active, inclusive family, so they cannot really be considered single. Many singles become friends with Poly-O Families and eventually trade in their single status for membership in the family, since a group relationship, as mentioned before, provides a good balance between time alone and membership in a loving group. Or a single person might become an "adjunct member" of an open Poly-O Family by dating one of the family members.

The Poly-L Triad is often made up of a married couple and a legally single person, but a Triad is definitely a family, so no member functions as a single person. Triad members experience all the inclusiveness and connection of any other person in a committed relationship, whether legally married or not. The Non-Triadic V-shaped Poly-L is quite a different story. Often all three members of a Non-Triadic Poly-L are single, which may be one reason it is one of the most fluid and least stable of the poly formations. Or a Poly-L may be made up of a married or committed couple, one of whom has an independent outside relationship with a single person. As mentioned before, a position on the outside vector of a Poly-L is a satisfactory role for a single person if that person wants limited commitment, a considerable amount of time alone, does not desire sexual interaction every day, or is involved in an engrossing career which provides the major passion in their life, but still wants some love and romance as well. As for the vertex of a Poly-L, this can be a good place for a single (or married) person who likes to feel needed, and wants to split time and energy without the commitment of a collaborative relationship, but doesn't want to spread energy around quite as much as a Poly-Porcupine may choose to do.

The Poly-Y is an excellent place for single people, as they are part of a larger network without having to be as intensely linked to the group as they would be in a Poly-O Family. The dynamics of their life are primarily influenced by their immediate intimate connections, yet they have communication with a large group of like-minded people who are there for them to discuss things with if they want, to celebrate life's joys, and to support them in times of need—all things which many single people miss and crave.

The ends of a Poly-S may be good places for singles, as this position provides them with a connection to a larger loving social group and an ongoing connection to one special person, yet time alone and much of the freedom of the single life.

Which form of poly is best for me?

So whether you are currently single, dating, in a committed monogamous relationship, or already in a polyamorous relationship, how do you go about looking at the options and starting to dream and plan for your future? I love that old song from South Pacific that says, "You gotta have a dream, if you don't have a dream, how you gonna make a dream come true?"

Your first step is to take an honest look at your personal dreams, fantasies, values, and lifestyle desires. As you read the descriptions of the various types of poly formations, which ones rocked your boat, warmed your heart, sounded exciting or cozy? And which ones sounded too weird to contemplate, too lonely, too complicated, too crowded, or just plain too much work?

Reflect on how you like to spend time. How much time do you like to spend alone? When with others, how often do you prefer to be with just one person, as a pair of friends and/or lovers? And how much do you like spending time as an integral part of a small group of good friends, or in a large group of friends? What about sex and sensuality? Do you love the idea of sharing sex in a threesome, foursome, or moresome? Or does that sound confusing, not very intimate, or maybe even a bit embarrassing? Does a puppy pile sound like something nobody over seven years old would do? Or does the thought of a big group cuddle turn you on?

What about communication? Is it the price you pay to get into the sack, a necessity you have to deal with in order to have relationships, an integral part of your life, the core joy of intimacy, or something you absolutely couldn't live without? The more members you have in an intimate group, the more communication you will want and need.

Now to a key factor, decision-making. In all forms of poly, members have more freedom than if they were in a traditional monogamous marriage, but less than they would have in a totally uncommitted single life. So where are you between these two extremes? One concept that is central to polyamory is that no one person is likely to meet all your needs. But when looking for another partner, how much do you want to focus on just your own needs as opposed to looking at the needs of your existing partner(s) or family members? If you place a high value on individuality, personal freedom, and unilateral decision-making, then the Poly-P Porcupine model will be ideal for you. If, on the other hand, you don't like operating as a lone ranger and long to be part of a collaborative family, you may be a candidate for a Poly-O Family. If you like intimacy and collaboration, but with a small group, perhaps a Poly-L Triad is your cup of tea.

Of course, life and romance often simply find us, and you may find yourself falling in love with a handsome stranger, only to discover that they are already an active part of a widespread Poly-Y Tribe. So you may suddenly find yourself drawn into a sensuous network that is bigger and better than you could have dreamed of creating. So be open to serendipity! However, knowing who you are, what you value, and where you dream of eventually finding yourself will prevent many wrong turns and a lot of wasted romantic energy.

Tips for collaborative decision-making

One colleague suggested that I add a few words about ways of reaching consensus decisions with a partner or small group. There are many books devoted to consensus decision-making, so I'll only mention a few things that I've found useful. First, don't wait until important issues come up, like choosing a new partner, to start practicing collaborative decision-making. If you're already accustomed to sharing your wishes and desires, listening to the wants of your partner(s) with an open mind, and working together to find something that works for everyone on topics like what to have for dinner or how to spend free time together, it's easier to agree on the big issues as well.

The first step is to speak for yourself rather than trying to guess what the other person wants. I remember the silly little "Where shall we go for dinner?" arguments I used to have with my husband when we were first married. "I know you love steak, sweetie, so let's go to that funky little steakhouse near the university." "But you've been talking about how long it's been since we've had Chinese, lover." Recognize that one? An hour later, we were still undecided and by then were starving, so tended to just thaw out a pizza, which made neither of us very happy.

We finally happened upon what we called the Rock, Paper, Scissors solution. Our model wasn't quite like the traditional scissors cut paper, paper covers rock, etc. But it was a still fun way to make decisions. This is how it went: "Where shall we go to dinner?" "I'm up for steak." "That would be okay, but I have a craving for Chinese." "OK, let's do Rock, Paper, Scissors." We'd take a minute to decide how strongly we craved steak or Chinese on a scale of one to five. Then on the count of three, we simultaneously put down our fist with the number of fingers out that indicated the strength of our craving. If I had mentioned steak, but it was a really weak preference and Chinese also sounded good, I might put out just one or two fingers. If I had a really serious craving for Chinese, I might put out four or five fingers. The strongest craving won, and we went for Chinese. But we each kept a small jar of chits or pennies for this game, and the person who had gotten their wish took a chit out of their jar and put it into the jar of the other person. The next time we played, if it came out a tie, one or the other of us could "sell" the other one of their chits to break the tie. It was all a game, but it saved lots of time, and prevented evenings from being spent eating yucky frozen pizza.

The same type of technique can be used with investigating more important desires, like how we prefer to spend our free time. "I like dancing and you like movies" could become a polarizing issue in a relationship. But there are probably many other things that two people both like doing. Try sitting down with your partner(s) and making a joint list of all kinds of things that one or more of you enjoy. Then individually, give each item your own personal preference rating:

> 3 I have a mad passion for doing this.
> 2 I enjoy this activity.
> 1 I like doing it once in a while.
> 0 It's okay. I don't have any strong positive or negative feelings about it.
> -1 I don't mind doing it, but seldom choose it.
> -2 I really don't enjoy it, but I might do it just to be with you.
> -3 I'd rather eat rotten eggs.

The same jar of chits can be used to "purchase" activities. If I really want to do something that is a 3 for me but a 0 for my partner and we agree to do it together, I contribute 3 chits to their jar. If they want one of their 3's and it's a 2 for me, it only costs them 1 chit. We generally agree to never attempt to buy something that is a -3 for our partner, but to just do that activity on our own or with another friend. This can be quite fun, and it not only keeps a balance between who gets to engage in their favorite activities, but also allows the other partners to stretch and become more comfortable with activities they might seldom choose. Furthermore, it prevents polarization around our favorite activities, or getting into the "we always do what *you* want to do!" routine.

Another game we played was betting time. We could gamble on most anything: "I'll bet these groceries are gonna add up to nearly $50!" "I'll wager you a half hour that they won't come to a cent over $45." Whoever wins gets to "bank" the time, to be collected at a time that is mutually agreeable to both parties (or more than one party if several are playing.) "I've won two hours, and I'd like to know if I can collect on Sunday morning from 9 to 11 am." Once the time is agreed upon, the winner is "King/Queen for the hour" and can request whatever they want. "I want you to start by serving me breakfast in bed—some of your fantastic scrambled eggs, wheat toast with jam, orange juice, and coffee, and place a small vase of freshly picked wildflowers on the tray, please. You are to play your guitar and sing to me as I eat my royal feast. Then you are to remove the tray, as well as my clothing, and starting with my feet…" I leave the rest to your imagination and creativity! This game can be a great way of learning to ask for what you want, in all kinds of fun ways, and to enjoy giving your partner(s) exactly what they want without trying to read their mind. And since it's pretty likely that partners win and lose an equal number of times, everyone gets to be pampered once in a while!

See how much fun playful decision-making can be? It is really important to learn that it's okay to ask for what we want. The first step in all these games is to look inside, when addressing both the frivolous and serious aspects of life, and to figure out what we really *do* want. As we get used to asking for what we want, as well as experiencing the joy of giving our partner(s) what they want, we expand our own experiences by trying new foods, new free time activities, and perhaps some wild, new sensuous activities which our royalty of the day requests. By starting with silly things like dinners, free time, and betting games, we get comfortable expressing our desires and responding to those of our partner(s). Then, when we discuss bigger issues, like what house to buy, whether or not to add new partners to our lives, or whether or not to have children, we've learned to trust that we will be heard, respected, listened to, and that reaching consensus can actually be fun.

Another hint to achieving positive decision-making skill is to follow the ancient Greek maxim, "Know Thyself!" I'm a certified Myers-Briggs trainer, and have presented a number of workshops at national poly conferences on using the personality type awareness provided by the Myers Briggs Type Indicator for building strong poly families. Understanding each member's innate preferences, the way they see the world, and how their personality type interfaces with that of other family members is incredibly valuable, in workplace teams, traditional marriages, and groups of all types, which is one reason Myers-Briggs is the most widely-used tool of its type in the world. The need for this type of awareness increases exponentially with the number of members in the team or family, making it a great asset for poly folks. There are a number of other tools out there to help you know yourself better, to be able to make clearer personal decisions, and to understand and respect the diverse styles within your family or intimate network. Looking inward and having the tools and vocabulary to describe what you find is important for everyone, and essential for people building poly relationships.

Back to relationship choices, one final note: don't sit on a shelf with your book of dreams on your lap, waiting for the perfect poly formation to fall down your chimney! We all know the old "better to have loved and lost" bit, as well as "you gotta kiss a lot of frogs…" My friend Ken Haslam likes to warn people that "there is a lot of poly roadkill on the way to polyamorous bliss!" Of course, he is right. So don't give up if at first you don't succeed. Love shared is never love wasted, so long as it is shared honestly and openly, with joy and juiciness and a genuine desire to learn and grow. Some of my best memories are of ill-fated short-term romances with men I'd never seriously contemplate creating family with. But each of them taught me something about myself, about love, about what I needed in a relationship – and about what I could not abide. Just because my very first romance didn't work, I didn't toss out the entire concept of romance.

The same is true of poly relationships. If the first one doesn't work, don't conclude that the entire concept simply doesn't work. Look how many people have tried monogamy for years, and after a divorce or two (or three or four) they keep trying the same relationship pattern again and again to see if this time they'll get it right. If your first poly relationship doesn't work, try a different model, different people, or simply find out what didn't work and do it differently the next time. And if, after trying poly for as long as you may have tried mono, you still find that poly isn't for you, there's always the option of going right back and trying monogamy again. Or the joys of the single world are still a valid option. This book is all about options, and about the fact that they are all equally valuable, so long as they are honest and fulfilling.

I used to have a poster on my office wall that said, "Blessed are those who dream dreams, and are willing to pay the price to make them reality." Yes, there are definitely prices involved in building a poly relationship, just as there are in forming any honest, caring relationship, be it monogamy, parenthood, or responsible non-monogamy. All of these require courage, self-awareness, willingness to take on societal pressure and inner insecurities, lots of trial and error, commitment to social change, and gobs of deep communication.

Don't forget that the most important relationship is the one you have with yourself. Start by forming a loving, caring relationship with yourself. Many of us also want to reach out and share what we find inside ourselves with someone else, to find intimate relationships with people who care and accept us as we are, while challenging us to become all we might be.

So join me in the wild, wonderful quest for love and laughter, joy and juiciness, sunshine and sex, fun and family! Go forth and be truthful, speak your mind, ask for what you want, give what you honestly can share, and follow your dreams.

Chapter 9

Time for Fun

Celebrations, Ceremonies and Surprises

Time for Fun
Celebrations, Ceremonies and Surprises

Has all this talk about agreements and communication started to make polyamory, and relationships in general, sound like all work and no play? Anything worth having takes work, and developing any type of loving partnership, be it monogamous or polyamorous, is worth the work and energy required. Without fun and pleasure, however, even the best communication will not succeed in making relationships work. All too many families allow the spark of joy and ecstasy to grow dim over time, or they lose it altogether. However, poly families find that not only does the need for positive communication increase exponentially with the number of people in a relationship, but so does the potential for love, laughter and fun. So our final chapter offers you few ideas to help keep the joy and vibrancy of poly relationships alive.

Let's have a date

Sheer busyness is the enemy of ecstasy. We schedule time for dentist's appointments, school conferences, meetings with our tax accountant. Is time with those we love less important to our health and well-being? A poly couple I know schedules one day a month on their calendar for a "Sensuous Day." Then when a call to an important meeting at church, a notice of a valuable professional seminar, or an invitation to a fun-sounding party comes up, each gets the same response: "Gosh, we're sorry but we already have a commitment for that day." Sometimes they invite outside lovers to join them for their celebration of sensuality, and sometimes the day involves just the two of them. But the format is always the same: all phones are turned off, especially sensuous food is prepared in advance, an erotic playlist is created for the iPod to play over the house-wide sound system, the hot tub is ready, and a romantic fire is burning in the fireplace. There may be a big mattress prepared in the living room in front of the fire, complete with pillows, toys, fruit, beverages, and whatever else will set the stage for a celebration of sensuality. Candles are lit, and an opening ritual transports the participants into sensuous space. The entire day is spent enjoying the love and ecstasy that is the heartbeat of their relationship.

Many lovers schedule romantic dates at least once a month, times to dress up and have a special evening as a pair, Triad, or entire family. They may to go out to dinner at a good restaurant, go dancing, attend a play or opera, drive to the mountains, take a romantic walk in the moonlight, or have a picnic in the park. What they do does not matter as much the attitude of importance and excitement that accompanies it. Setting aside time to go out on dates with one's regular partner(s) is a vital part of the ongoing courtship process. These outings are just as sexy and exciting as a first date with a shiny new potential love object. When we stop courting our partner(s), the relationship starts going stale.

Surprise me!

Surprises are another way to add fun and spontaneity to relationships and combat the deadly dullness of routine life. Creativity is more important than cost when it comes to the wonderful magic of surprise. One of my friends got a phone call at work one morning announcing an emergency lunch meeting at a nearby office address. When she arrived, two of her partners grabbed her as she walked through the door, blindfolded her, locked the office door, and placed her spread-eagle on the table of the small conference room. There they fed her mystery foods: fruits, candy, vegetables interspersed with surprises like a slice of lemon or piece of ice. They teased her nose with aromatic plants like lavender, mint, sage, and rosemary, and brushed away the stress of her day with a large feather duster. An after-lunch massage finished off the surprise. Of course, the partners had planned ahead and reserved the conference room for an exclusive meeting with a special client. Otherwise there might have been a rather unwelcome surprise during the course of the luncheon…

One fun-loving poly family has created their own Fantasy Island game. All the members write down several silly or serious but achievable fantasy ideas on little pieces of paper and put them all into an oatmeal box. Once a month, every member pulls a slip of paper, folds it carefully away where nobody else can read it, and creates a plan for enacting that fantasy for an individual or group of members of the family sometime during the month, preferably when least expected. Of course, if the fantasy selected doesn't fit the style or ability of the person who drew it, they may create an even better one. The fantasies may be silly, like coming home from work to find one's room totally decorated in balloons. They may be sensuous, like being treated to an eight-handed massage. They might be practical, like being relieved from house duties for an entire week, or being fed a special meal. Or they may be kinky, like being blindfolded and taken someplace outdoors, tied to a tree, and played with by the entire family with the possible assistance of trusted friends. For those who want a little outside inspiration, there are sets of fantasy cards available in erotic shops or online. But the great advantage of creating your own is that it encourages each family member to look inside, find and express their own all-too-often hidden dreams!

My partner, the sexy sailor man, is a genius at surprises, especially when I'm returning home from a trip. One time, at the end of a very long flight, he was at the airport to meet me holding several big balloons. He'd put fresh rose petals in a small plastic bag with a ripcord, and this surprise bag was held up and hidden by the other balloons. When I emerged from customs, he threw his arms around me while pulling the ripcord, and rose petals showered down all over me! You should have heard the "ohhs" and "ahhs" from my fellow passengers.

Another time, he was at the airport all dressed up in a suit and tie (not at all his regular attire) holding a sign like those used by representatives from hotels who are there to meet guests. It had a lovely picture of our yard and hot tub, and in large letters said: "Dr. Mim Chapman—Welcome to Santa Fe Heaven, the Ultimate Pleasure Spa." He greeted me with courtesy and respect, as if I were an important visiting dignitary, and escorted me quite formally to his waiting car, which had rose petals strewn over the passenger seat. When we got home, he told me to wait in the car until he called me on my cell phone to tell me my accommodations were ready.

When my phone rang inviting me into my special spa, dozens of votive candles lined the entrance hall. He had lit a pre-prepared fire in the fireplace, put on classical music, and the massage table was set up just to the left of the roaring fire. My gracious host met me at the door naked except for an apron and chef hat. He bowed and said, "Welcome to Santa Fe Heaven, the Ultimate Pleasure Spa, where your wish is my command." There was a martini waiting for me on a tray by the fireplace, along with some lovely finger foods. Needless to say, the service at Santa Fe Heaven Pleasure Spa definitely lived up to the description on the welcome flier!

Everything calls for a celebration

Celebrations are another necessary part of family life. Of course, the more members in a family, the more birthdays there are to celebrate. But it's even more fun to create celebrations that are totally unexpected because they don't happen on the same date each year. There are so many things to celebrate, if you keep your eyes open for them. Five days of sunshine in a row may call for a naturist celebration in which everyone rolls naked in the grass in the sunshine, that is, if you have a very private back yard or can go to a secluded mountain meadow nearby. Five days of rain may call for a communal rain dance in the shower together. If a family rotates cooking chores, a fantastic dinner might be celebrated by giving the chef a surprise group massage. The arrival of a tax refund check calls for an orgy of tiny special food treats, possibly served on the naked body of the member who received the check. Any bit of good news on the evening news can call for a spontaneous, immediate "puppy pile" group cuddle right there in front of the television.

Celebrations and parties are all about keeping the inner child alive, and the fun-loving inner child loves playing with fantasy. Once in the middle of the long, dark Alaskan winter, I closed all the drapes to block out the cold and the sight of the fiercely blowing snow, turned the thermostat up as high as it would go, and put Indonesian gamelan music on the stereo. When my tiny home had become toasty warm, I spread a beach towel on the living room floor, put on my bikini, fixed a tall drink and went to Bali for the afternoon! The beach party would have been even more fun if I'd had an intimate family to toss beach balls with and dance with me in the sand. But I brought them all to the beach in my fantasy. And where did I find sand when the ground outside was covered with five feet of snow? Clean kitty litter did the trick, of course. I celebrated a lovely although solitary afternoon lying in the sand on my fantasy beach in Bali, and having really hot private sex under the Indonesian sun!

In addition to fun or silly celebrations, there are also more serious rituals that can add joy and meaning to family life. Some families do ribbon tying ceremonies to welcome a new member into the group, using various colored ribbons to create a symbolic communal web of love and safety with the new member in the center of the web. Baptisms in the hot tub can also be wonderful ritual celebrations.

Endings are as important to celebrate as beginnings, yet they are all-too-often overlooked. If a member leaves a relationship, it's a good time to create a going-away ceremony, telling stories about the fun times everybody has shared, the lessons they've learned from each other, presenting the departing member with little symbolic mementos of the love they've shared, and ending the ritual by writing down hopes and wishes for the departing member's future, as well as for the future of those remaining in the family.

Changes in family status also call for ceremonies or rituals. Morphing from one form of poly to another is a cause for celebration. A graduation, new baby, new job, raise, new hat, new hair color—you name it and there's a celebration waiting to happen.

Many people use ritual to facilitate and celebrate change. One author I read years ago stated, "True change only happens in ritual space." I've forgotten the author, but not the idea. I'm not sure change *only* happens in ritual space, but I do believe that rituals can be important ways of nurturing and celebrating inner change. We can learn a lot from the primal cultures who used ritual in a wide variety of ways, both to facilitate personal change and to build group cohesiveness.

Some families use rituals from the traditions of their own or other faith communities, often choosing them from a wide variety of cultures, and sometimes modifying them to meet their own needs. Some poly families follow the Pagan spiritual path and find within it a wealth of ceremonies to use for both ritual and celebration. Others simply create rituals of their own. To find examples of ceremonies and rituals especially tailored to the unique needs of poly families, check out Raven Kaldera's *Pagan Polyamory*.

Turning practical actions into rituals helps keep the magic in everyday life. Remember that song from South Pacific, "I'm Gonna Wash That Man Right Outa My Hair"? That is a great example of using a routine daily event as a ritual to cleanse yourself from the pain of a frustrating relationship. A friend of mine uses housecleaning as a ritual for getting rid of stress in her life. On each stroke of the broom or vacuum, she chants, "Away with this mess, anger and stress, clean up my nest, worry a lot less!" Create your own mantra, or use a traditional one like "Om Mani Padme Hum," which may be the most widely used mantra in the world.

By the way, here's a tidbit guaranteed to put a special Buddha smile on your face while you're chanting this age-old mantra. While in Dharamsala last year, I spent quite a bit of time studying in the library created by the Dalai Lama, who lives in exile in this beautiful mountain town in northern India. One of the most fascinating books I read was *Traveller in Space, In Search of Female Identity in Tibetan Buddhism,* by June Campbell, a Scottish scholar who has studied Tibetan Buddhism in the monasteries of India since the early 1970's. It contained her research into the meaning of Om Mani Padme Hum.

"Hail to the jewel in the lotus," is the most common translation of this ancient mantra. Most think this refers to an image of the Buddha sitting on a lotus. If you are interested in eastern mythology, you know that the lotus is a symbol for the female or her *yoni.* The word *jewel* is sometimes used to refer to the *lingam* or penis, so the mantra could also be interpreted as meaning, "Hail to the penis in the vagina." Not a bad image to use for meditation!

But this female Tantric scholar said that the Sanskrit ending of the word for *jewel* in the mantra is actually female, not male. So she proposes that the "jewel in the lotus" refers not to the Buddha, nor to the *lingam* in the *yoni,* but to the clitoris, the jewel of the *yoni*! Don't you love the thought of millions of people all over the world meditating while chanting "Hail to the clit"? That thought should make meditation rituals way more juicy!

Back to the subject of rituals to celebrate life changes. Of course, poly marriage is not legal, and I don't expect it to become so during my lifetime. But some Unitarian Universalist ministers offer commitment ceremonies for poly partners. There are also Pagan ceremonies, based on the handfasting tradition, that can be used by polys who wish to publicly formalize their partnerships.

There are all kinds of other life changes that can be celebrated through creative ritual ceremonies: decade birthdays; graduations and other completions and endings; new jobs, lovers, homes, cars, boats, toys; menopause; retirement; the list is limited only by your creativity!

Some polys consider fluid-bonding (condomless sex) to be an emotional and spiritual bond, not just the result of physical testing and the necessary wait period. They see being fluid-bonded as symbolizing a deeper, more intimate commitment. In my last Triad, in which I was the third and newest partner, we created a ceremony to welcome me into the family as a fluid-bonded member and a co-primary. At the time, I lived in Alaska and my two partners lived on the east coast. My male partner met me in Colorado to start looking for a place we might want to relocate so we could all be together.

Our other partner couldn't take time off from work, so she was still back east. Since our relationship had progressed to the point where we were contemplating living together, we were moving to a more intimate commitment. On the physical side, we'd all been tested, the wait period was over, and we were anxious to get rid of condoms. The two of us went to Boulder, where there is a large poly community, and asked them to help us celebrate our fluid-bonding ceremony, with our third member participating from the Philly area, where she was working. How's that for a less-than-traditional setting for an important ceremony?

With the permission of my two partners, Lee Hencen and Pete Benson, and of *Loving More* magazine which published our fluid-bonding ceremony in their Winter 2006 edition, I'd like to share this simple ritual as a sample of what you can create for your own family. What better way to end a book than with a ritual for beginning a more intimate poly relationship?

May you create, change, laugh, love, celebrate and continue to grow together through forming the families of your dreams, and celebrating life with creativity and zest!

Fluid-Bonding Ceremony

by Mim Chapman, Lee Hencen, and Pete Benson

August 12, 2002

Props:

A condom, unrolled; 3 candles; butane lighter or matches; any other decorations desired; a pair of scissors; a bottle of wine or water; a nice pottery cup; background music; video camera; cell phone.

Preparations:

Decide in advance who will light the candles; who stands where; who will read each portion of text; who will hold the condom up; who will cut it; who will pour the wine or water into the cup; the order of sipping from the cup. Just before the ceremony, after the candles are lit, Mim and Pete call Lee on the cell phone. The cell phone is clipped to Mim's or Pete's clothing so it will pick up both voices well enough for Lee to hear.

Participants take turns reading portions of the following text:

Water is the material basis of all life, from microbes to humans. Not only do our bodies consist mostly of water, but also each of our watery bodies serves as a vast oceanic home for countless microscopic organisms, some symbiotically beneficial to us, some harmful. Human ingenuity has devised physical barriers [hold up the condom] to stop the spread of the harmful microbes.

But life is more than just separate specks of consciousness swimming in a watery medium. Human life is not about barriers or separateness; it is about connecting, joining, sharing, loving. We three have come to love each other deeply, and it is natural for us to express our mutual love physically as deeply and directly as is possible.

Therefore, as the three of us overlap the individual boundaries of our lives, physically, intellectually, emotionally and spiritually, and having determined that we are sufficiently free of the harmful microbes, it is fitting that we should also merge the watery essence of our bodies. And so we now sever this physical barrier that has heretofore separated our bodily fluids.

One person holds the condom up, grasping each end so it is taut. The other takes the scissors and cuts the condom into two pieces. Lee cuts her condom also, back in Philly, where she is participating via cell phone. After condom pieces and the scissors are set down, some wine or water is poured into the cup.

We now recite together: *Now we share this cup of wine as a symbol of our shared fluids, our shared love, our shared life. And, as we enter this new phase of our relationship, may our thoughts, dreams, ideas, fantasies, fears, needs, wishes and plans for the future also flow freely between us without barriers of dishonesty, hesitancy or fear of rejection. May we continue to grow in love and life.*

We sip from the cup in turn, while both together hold the cup and while Lee also shares a cup of wine with us on her end of the phone. The cup is set down, and we kiss and hug (including Lee via phone.) We thank the guests from the poly network in Boulder for joining us in our celebration. We then carry the candles into the bedroom, lovingly remove each other's clothing, share any further conversation desired with Lee before hanging up the phone, and proceed to exercise our new condom-free sexual status for the first time.

Amen, Shalom, Namaste, and Blessed Be!

Acknowledgments

Many of us were once out there alone, wondering if we were the only people in the world who longed to create a family that was quite different from that of our parents. This book is the result of some of us being able to find each other, share dreams and experiences, and learn from each other. So I am deeply indebted to all the polyamorous or poly-curious people I've met at conferences, discussion groups, social gatherings, or online who openly shared their joys and frustrations, hopes and desires, problems and successes as they build their own unique relationships. These brave poly folks are some of the pioneers of our times. Although poly is not a new way of loving, it is considered radical within our somewhat conservative Western society. So I want to start by thanking all these people whose courage and honesty form the basis of this book.

I want to thank the leaders in the poly community who have done a great service to all of us by enabling us to find each other. Robyn Trask with Loving More works incredibly hard to organize the wonderful Loving More and Poly Living conferences that enable us to meet and share ideas. These conferences have brought me in contact with more wonderful poly presenters than I could possibly mention. Some of the ones who have had a special influence on me are Dr. Ken Haslam who founded the Polyamory Archive Collection at the Kinsey Institute, Indiana University, and Dr. Dave Hall, who has been a poly leader for years. If you haven't attended a Loving More conference, do so! You can find information about national and local conferences at lovemore.com. And be sure to read their magazine, Loving More, which has been in existence for over 20 years.

Another national organization I want to acknowledge is Unitarian Universalists for Polyamory Awareness (UUPA). Its website, uupa.org, includes valuable information about polyamory, including copies of sermons on the topic that have been presented in various UU churches across the nation and information about local chapters of UUPA. I am proud to be a member of the only faith community I know of that has an organization to support poly folks and help ministers and congregations understand and welcome poly families. Thanks to the officers and members of UUPA for the great work they are doing for poly folks everywhere, and for their personal support as I grew in my poly lifestyle.

Three Alaskan friends deserve special thanks for their support during my early "coming out" days. Dr. Fred Hillman and Jackie Buckley, two leaders in the Anchorage GLBT community, were the first people to whom I came out as poly. They had never heard the word before, but supported my first scary steps in accepting, exploring and sharing my identity. Pat Wendt was the first and the only other poly person I met in Alaska. Finding him was like finding water in the desert! He nurtured and supported me in my poly growth, and will always be a love and an important member of my poly family.

How could I have been so lucky as to have met Lee Hencen and Pete Benson at my first Tri-State Poly meeting in New York City, and eventually fallen in love with them? Lee and Pete are not only amazing people and active leaders in the poly community, but they also taught me how effective open communication is in building a poly relationship. Pete has recently written his own book about poly, *The Polyamory Handbook*. Lee leads numerous workshops at poly gatherings and is still my "poly sister" and dearest friend. She and my other long-term friend, Shari Deghi, were with me when I first thought of writing this book. They helped give birth to its basic concepts, and have been guiding lights throughout its formation. Thanks to you, Shari, for always being there for me, and thanks to both of you, Pete and Lee, for being my first poly mentors.

Each one of my loves, long-term or short-term, taught me something about relationships. Without naming you, I want each of you to know you are valued, loved, and appreciated! This book is the result of all you have taught me.

The members of the Northern New Mexico Polyamory Network, which meets at my house monthly, have been a constant source of inspiration and support. They invited me to do an overview of the book at one of our meetings, and gave me valuable feedback, suggestions, and additional ideas.

Huge thanks to several of my dear friends who volunteered to read and edit for me. Dr. Fred Hillman, Hansa Krijgsman, Matthew C. Cox, Susan Hall, Pete Benson, Sera Miles, Bugs Papastathis, Julie Gray, Jo Swiss, Dr. Dave Hall, Lee Hencen, and Dr. Atsushi Tajima dedicated hours of their time to reading, proofing, editing, and giving feedback. T.A. and Al contributed creative assistance with graphics and layout. Without the combined genius of these friends, this book would not have been possible.

Thanks also to Hansa Krijgsman, Roark Barron and Mistress Kitten for their help in finding gender-neutral names for use in the relationship examples. Since polyamorous relationships may be gay, bi or straight, I did not want to use gender-specific names. Initially, I used letters of the alphabet to represent people. But my partner, who hates math, said that looked way too much like algebra! So, with the help of these friends, I found non-gendered names to replace the letters. I hope this helps make the examples clear, yet applicable to all types of affectional orientations.

Finally, my greatest thanks goes to my current primary partner, John "Bugs" Papastathis. He is one of the kindest, most nurturing people I have ever met, and has fully supported me in working on this book, encouraging me to openly share examples from our own relationship, not only the joys, but also the challenges. I hope that sharing our tough times, yet knowing that we're still together, will give you hope when you're going through challenges with your partner(s). A huge hug, kiss and snuggle full of appreciation to my dear Bugs for his patience, love and support! We are dedicated to helping each other achieve our individual and rather different poly dreams, and share a juicy mixture of love, flexibility, and genuine celebration of polydiversity!

Polyamory Resources

Anapol, Deborah, <u>Polyamory, The New Love Without Limits: Secrets of Sustainable Intimate Relationships</u>. 1997.

Anderlini-D'Onofrio, Serena, <u>Eros: A Journey of Multiple Loves</u>. 2006.

Anderlini-D'Onofrio, Serena & Klein, Fritz, <u>Plural Loves: Designs for Bi and Poly Living</u>. 2005.

Baker, Robin, <u>Sperm Wars: The Science of Sex</u>. 1996

Barash, David & Lipton, Judith, <u>The Myth of Monogamy: Fidelity and Infidelity in Animals and People</u>. 2002.

Benson, Peter, <u>The Polyamory Handbook: A User's Guide</u>. 2008.

Block, Jenny, <u>Open: Love, Sex and Life in an Open Marriage</u>. 2009.

Carrallas, Bargara & Sprinkle, Annie, <u>Urban Tantra: Sacred Sex for the Twenty-First Century</u>. 2007.

Easton, Dossie & Hardy, Janet, <u>The Ethical Slut: A Practical Guide to Polyamory, Open Relationships and Other Adventures</u>. 2009.

Foster, Barbara and Michael & Hadady, Letha, <u>Three In Love: Ménages à Trois from Ancient to Modern Times</u>. 1997.

Graff, E.J., <u>What is Marriage For? The Strange Social History of our Most Intimate Institution</u>. 2004.

Gruber, Tom, <u>What the Bible "Really" Says About Sex: A New Look at Sexual Ethics from a Biblical Perspective</u>. 2006.

Heinlein, Kris & Rozz, <u>The Sex and Love Handbook: Polyamory! Bisexuality! Swingers! Spirituality! (& even Monogamy!) A Practical Optimistic Relationship Guide</u>. 2004.

Heinlein, Robert, <u>Stranger in a Strange Land</u>. 1961.

Kaldera, Raven, <u>Pagan Polyamory: Becoming a Tribe of Hearts</u>. 2005.

Kraft, Isa, <u>Split-Self</u>. 2009.

Lessin, Janet, <u>Polyamory, Many Loves: The Poly-Tantric Lovestyle, A Personal Account</u>. 2006.

Ley, David, <u>Insatiable Wives: Women Who Stray and the Men Who Love Them</u>. 2009.

Matik, Wendy-O, <u>Redefining Our Relationships: Guidelines for Responsible Open Relationships</u>. 2002.

Mazur, Ronald, <u>The New Intimacy: Open-Ended Marriage and Alternative Lifestyles</u>. 2000.

McGarey, Robert, <u>Poly Communication Survival Kit: The Essential Tools for Building and Enhancing Relationships</u>. 1999.

Members of the Kerista Commune, <u>Polyfidelity: Sex in the Kerista Commune and Other Related Theories on How to Solve the World's Problems</u>. 1984.

Munson, Marcia & Stelboum, Judith, <u>The Lesbian Polyamory Reader: Open Relationships, Non-Monogamy, and Casual Sex</u>. 1999.

Mystic Life, <u>Spiritual Polyamory</u>. 2003.

Naisbitt, John, <u>Megatrends</u>. 1982.

O'Neill, Nena & George, <u>Open Marriage</u>. 1972.

Parker, Christina, <u>Many Hearts, Many Loves, Many Possibilities: The Polyamory Relationship Workbook</u>. 2009.

Ravenscroft, Anthony, <u>Polyamory: Roadmaps for the Clueless & Hopeful</u>. 2004.

Rimmer, Robert, <u>The Harrad Experiment</u>. 1962.

Sharman, Anna, <u>Open Fidelity: An A-Z Guide</u>. 2006.

Taormino, Tristan, <u>Opening Up: A Guide to Creating and Sustaining Open Relationships</u>. 2008.

Walker, Rebecca, <u>One Big Happy Family: Eighteen Writers Talk About Polyamory, Open Adoption, Mixed Marriage, Househusbandry, Single Motherhood, and Other Realities of Truly Modern Love</u>. 2009.

Websites

Loving More Non-Profit—an international organization that sponsors conferences, workshops, a poly magazine, and links to lots of other poly sites: http://www.lovemore.com

Polyamory Meetup Groups—access local poly groups: http://polyamory.meetup.com

Polyamorous Percolations—a resource for people in poly relationships or curious about poly: http://polyamoryonline.org

Polyamory Society—resource materials and links to local groups: http://www. polyamorysociety.org

Polyamory in the Media—what's being written about polyamory: http://www. polyinthemedia.blogspot.com

Polychromatic—reviews of books about or related to polyamory: http://polychromatic.com

Practical Polyamory—downloadable documents with indepth info dealing with polyamorous relationships: http://www.practicalpolyamory.com

The World Polyamory Association—information and conferences: http:// worldpolyamoryassociation.org

Unitarian Universalists for Polyamory Awareness—resources, sermons on polyamory, and UU Polyamory local chapters: http://www.uupa.org

Poly Personals:
http://www.lovingmorepersonals.com exclusively for Loving More members
http://www.polyfriendfinder.com
http://www.polymatchmaker.com

About the author

Mim Chapman is an educator, a learner, and a change agent. She has been polyamorous her entire life, since well before the word itself was coined. Mim has presented keynotes and workshops at national and local poly conferences, including Poly Living and Loving More east and west. She is a national officer of Unitarian Universalists for Polyamory Awareness, and has given sermons on polyamory for Unitarian churches. She is a member of the Board of Directors of Loving More and the host of the New Mexico Polyamory Discussion Group.

Her work experience includes commercial fishing, civil rights activism, marine salvage, political lobbying and fundraising, and education. She has led three school restructuring projects, a lobbying effort which changed a major federal fisheries law, and created a series of women's seminars that led to the formation of the Cordova Family Resource Center.

She has taught at elementary to graduate school levels; been the director of a community college, the principal of a rural K-12 school and an urban, inner-city middle school; worked in large east coast urban schools and tiny Eskimo villages, from the Caribbean to Nova Scotia to Alaska. During the time she was Principal of Clark Middle School in Anchorage, Alaska, Clark was named one of four mid-level schools in the nation with the most innovative, successful programs to address diversity.

Mim is a certified Myers-Briggs trainer and has led workshops in various aspects of learning styles, multiple intelligences, collaboration, diversity, and the change process for conferences, schools and businesses. She was chosen the Alaska *Curriculum Leader of the Year*, Toastmaster's *Communicator of the Year*, and the YWCA/British Petroleum *Woman of Achievement*. She has a Bachelors Degree from St. Louis Institute of Music; a Masters from Washington University,

St. Louis; a Ph.D. from Mississippi State University; and a second Masters in Counseling and Guidance from University of Alaska Anchorage. She spent many years as a professor at University of Alaska. Her publications include workbooks, articles, and a textbook on school reform. She recently created and performed in her first theatre work, *The VP (vagina-penis) Dialogues,* a performance art piece based on her research into the status of sex education in our culture.

Mim offers relationship coaching in person and via phone, is an active sex educator, and travels extensively providing training, program development, future search retreats, executive mentoring, and other consulting services for business and education through her private consulting firm, **MIMCO** (mimco.org) whose letters indicate some of her work focuses:

Multicultural Understanding, Celebrating Diversity, Anti-Harassment Workshops
  Intimacy, Sexuality and Relationship Coaching in Person and via Phone
    Myers-Briggs Personality Types Workshops for Organizations and Individuals
      Creative Ceremonies for Marriage, Commitment, Divorce, other Life Passages
        Organizational Change, Future Search Retreats for Organizations and Schools

What is Polyamory?

How Can We Better
Understand, Welcome and Serve
Polyamorous Families and Individuals?

An Interactive Workshop for
Counselors, Therapists, Ministers, Social Workers, Educators
Churches, Health Providers, Businesses and Schools

A Curriculum Designed by Mim Chapman, PhD

author of *What Does Polyamory Look Like? Polydiverse Patterns of
Loving and Living in Modern Polyamorous Relationships*
and *WHAT IF? Rethinking Education*

**Curriculum Guide and Visual Materials for this Innovative Seminar available at
www.mimco.org**

WHAT IF?

Re-Thinking Education: A School Reformer's Guide

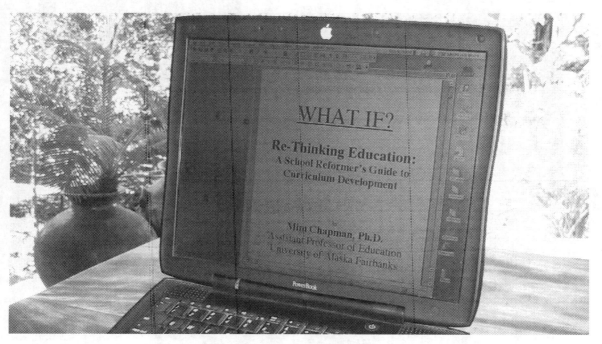

A Creative Handbook for
Parents, Students, Educators, Administrators
Politicians and Political Activists
and everyone interested in creating and supporting
more successful educational systems around the world

Mim Chapman, PhD

PhD in Educational Leadership and Counseling, MA in Counseling, Certified Myers-Briggs Trainer, teacher and retired principal, college professor, numerous workshops at conferences

Pictures from the Alaska Production of The VP (vagina-penis) Dialogues:

This thought-provoking, entertaining performance arts piece is based on the author's research into the success, or lack thereof, of sex education in our culture. Exact questions asked by hundreds of youth and adults are read onstage by the "Pubic Chorus," and responded to by the co-stars, Penis and Vagina!

Entrance of the chorus of pubic hairs in *The VP Dialogues*

Questions from the audience, written during intermission, are answered by a certified sex therapist in the post show talk-back. The production does not require trained actors, and takes very few rehearsals. If you're looking for a creative way to provide positive sex education in your community, church, or college, this just may be what you are looking for!

Basic Anatomy 101

Alaska cast of The VP Dialogues

Is "Just Say NO!" Enough to Know?

THE VP (vagina-penis) DIALOGUES

A Singing, Dancing, Entertaining
Sex Education Production for All Ages

Audience May Write Confidential Questions to be Answered During Post-Show Talk-Back!
What have you always wanted to ask about sex, and not had a safe place???

**A Positive, Factual yet Entertaining Comprehensive Sex Education
Performance Art Piece, Perfect for Churches, Colleges and Communities**

**Script, Performance Rights, and DVD of a Community Performance in Alaska
available at www.mimco.org**

Photo by Ludwig Laab

MIMCO

Multicultural Understanding, Celebrating Diversity, Anti-Harassment Workshops
Intimacy, Sexuality and Relationship Coaching in Person and via Phone
Myers-Briggs Personality Types Workshops for Organizations and Individuals
Creative Ceremonies for Marriage, Commitment, Divorce, other Life Passages
Organizational Change, Future Search Retreats for Organizations and Schools

www.mimco.org

Appointments for Relationship Coaching in Person or by Phone
Keynote Presentations and Workshops
Creation of Unique Ceremonies and Rituals
Books, Articles, Curriculum Guides
Educational Materials and Training Seminars

For these or related services or to share your own stories and feedback, contact Mim
Chapman at www.mimco.org

MIMCO
Santa Fe, New Mexico
mimco8@gmail.com